Praise for
Susan Cameron and
Perfecting Your English Pronun

"Susan Cameron has provided us the ultimate toolbox ... *rfecting Your English Pronunciation*. Students are newly baptized with such clarity of language with her outstanding text. Highly recommended for any non-native speaker needing to reduce their accent."

James Calleri, CSA
Associate Professor and Head of Acting, Theatre MFA Program
Columbia University School of the Arts

"Working with Susan and her book took my American accent to a new level and increased my confidence dramatically. It is an indispensable aid for anyone who is learning an American accent, and incredibly user-friendly"

Charlie Cox
British actor, star of Netflix/Marvel's Daredevil

"Susan Cameron is one of the pre-eminent voice instructors in the county. Her transformative technique is smart, practical and essential."

Pippin Parker
Dean, New School of Drama, MFA Program
Associate Dean, College of Performing Arts
New School University

"Susan worked with my two principal actresses in *Snow Flower and the Secret Fan*. She did accent reduction with them and helped them say their dialogue with more fluency. She was an experienced and creative coach."

Wayne Wang
Film director, *The Joy Luck Club*, *Maid in Manhattan*, and *Smoke*

"Susan Cameron's focus on difficult-to-speak sound combinations, extensive word lists highlighting English spelling patterns, and accompanying recordings which serve as a mini pronunciation dictionary, all make this book a must for speakers of English as a second language."

Patricia Fletcher
Associate Professor, New School for Drama
Author of *Classically Speaking*

"In my experience, there is no one more insightful and profoundly gifted. Students under her tutelage are radically transformed and become significantly more competitive in their fields."

Robert Lupone
Former Director, MFA Program, New School for Drama
New School University

"Susan sets a new standard for excellence in the field of ESL pronunciation. You won't find a better wealth of knowledge in a single source."

Dr. Pamelia Phillips
Author of *Singing for Dummies*

Perfecting Your
English
Pronunciation

Perfecting Your
English
Pronunciation

Second Edition

Susan Cameron

New York Chicago San Francisco Athens
London Madrid Mexico City Milan
New Delhi Singapore Sydney Toronto

1 2 3 4 5 6 7 8 9   LCR   23 22 21 20 19 18

ISBN   978-1-260-11702-8
MHID   1-260-11702-2

e-ISBN   978-1-260-11703-5
e-MHID   1-260-11703-0

Interior design by Village Bookworks, Inc.

McGraw-Hill Education books are available at special quantity discounts to
use as premiums and sales promotions, or for use in corporate training
programs. To contact a representative, please visit the Contact Us page at
www.mhprofessional.com.

McGraw-Hill Education Language Lab App

Extensive audio recordings and videos are available to support your study
of this book. Go to www.mhlanguagelab.com to access the web version of
this application, or to locate links to the mobile app for iOS and Android
devices. More details about the features of the app are available on the
inside front cover.

For all my students, past, present, and future,
and
in memory of my father, Harold T. MacDonald,
who instilled in me a passion for the English language

Contents

PART ONE
GETTING STARTED

ONE
Retraining the articulation muscles 3

TWO
The International Phonetic Alphabet 11

PART THREE
THE RHYTHMS OF ENGLISH

SEVENTEEN
Syllable stress within words 233

EIGHTEEN
Word stress within sentences 247

PART FOUR
PUTTING IT ALL TOGETHER

NINETEEN
Marking a business speech   259

Acknowledgments

I would like to thank the many people who have made this book, video recording, and audio recording set a reality. I am indebted to McGraw-Hill Education, and especially to my wonderful editors Holly McGuire (original edition) and Christopher Brown (revised edition) for guiding me through the process of publication. I am eternally grateful to my colleagues, who have taught me so much and who continue to inspire me daily, especially Patricia Fletcher and Deborah Hecht.

For the text of the book, I thank Patricia Fletcher and Nick Cianfrogna for their editing suggestions and input. Thanks, too, to those who helped me in the early writing, especially Sara Wolski, literary consultant extraordinaire; my sister Meg MacDonald, for editing support; Keith Buhl, for lending me his IPA font; Diego Galan, for assistance with the business text in Part Four; and Theodora P. Loukas, for compiling and typing the numerous word lists.

I am grateful to the talented people who helped create the video and audio recordings: Nick Cianfrogna for lending his terrific voice to the extensive word lists, and Mariah Cruz of Dubway Recording Studios for her impeccable sound engineering skills; Theodora P. Loukas, producer and director; Maggie Mei Lin, filmographer and editor; and Carlos Cano, Chih Hua Yeh, Wayne Liu, Dimitri Letsios, and Angelo Niakas. Special thanks to Anne Goulet, for the "Fred" artwork; Aaron Jodion, for the video music; and Eric Maltz, for editing and mixing the example sentence recordings. I am especially indebted to Theodora P. Loukas and Maggie Mei Lin for making the videos a reality.

I also thank my wonderful students who appear on the video and audio recordings: Nandita Chandra, Juan Carlos Infante, Vin Kridakorn, Yuki Akashi, Martina Potratz, and Vaishnavi Sharma.

Finally, thanks to all of my past students. You have been my inspiration and my greatest teachers.

Introduction

Fred skipped lunch that Monday afternoon. It wasn't because he was planning to leave the office early for his much anticipated first date with Carla, or that he was saving his appetite for their 7:15 P.M. dinner reservation at the hot new French bistro in the West Village. It wasn't even because of the extra serving of bacon he'd had at breakfast.

Fred skipped lunch because his stomach was churning, his pulse was racing, and his thoughts had begun to jumble. The CEO of Fred's company had flown into the city for a managerial meeting to discuss downsizing at the corporate level, and in an afternoon peppered with presentations, Fred was scheduled to speak first.

Fred was prepared. He was excited about the innovative cost-cutting methods he had devised. His PowerPoint slides were exquisite, his handouts polished, and his presentation of both was well rehearsed. But there was a problem: Fred had to deliver his speech in English, and English wasn't Fred's native tongue. Although Fred's expertise was clear, his pronunciation was not. He worried that if his words were not completely understood, his remarkable contribution would be undervalued.

Sound familiar? If you have picked up this book, it probably does.

Every day, millions of business professionals like you report to jobs dreading the possibility of not being understood. This has nothing to do with talent, skill, or advanced knowledge of the subject; it is because you must speak in the international language of English, and as a nonnative speaker, you have never learned precise pronunciation. This is understandable: When learning English as a second language, most students are taught primarily through reading and writing. What many ESOL classes do not emphasize, however, is that English is a *nonphonetic* language—its spelling patterns often seem to have little resemblance to its pronunciation. At best, this is puzzling; at worst, it can cost talented individuals their jobs.

Consider the words *stop, go,* and *other*; all three are spelled with the letter *o,* but each is pronounced with a different vowel *sound.* Thus, while you may be fluent in English—even a master of vocabulary—*speaking* English clearly and naturally may be difficult. You may also have been influenced by your own ESOL teachers' less-than-perfect pronunciation skills.

Compounding this difficulty is the fact that most languages do not have some of the sounds used in English. You may approximate these sounds, substituting a similar one from your native language, or you may pronounce a word according to the spelling patterns of your native tongue. Even among those speakers of languages that use the Latin alphabet, there is confusion: English has 24 vowel sounds, while most languages of Latin origin have far fewer. In addition, the anatomical placement of English sounds can be especially difficult for natives of Asian cultures, since many vowel and consonant sounds of English are realized much farther forward in the mouth and involve tongue positions not used in Asian languages.

Many Asian ESOL speakers have found success with the *Perfecting Your English Pronunciation* method. In September 1993, I received a telephone call from a diplomat with the Japanese consulate, asking if I might help Prime Minister Morihiro Hosokawa with his English pronunciation: He wanted to be the first Japanese prime minister ever to address the General Assembly of the United Nations in English. Of course, I agreed, and had the honor both to meet and work with the prime minister on his pronunciation and intonation. His English was excellent, and his attention to the nuances of pronunciation exceptional. His address before the General Assembly was, indeed, quite impressive.

Although few of us have to perform on such a public platform, excellent pronunciation is a valuable asset—indeed, a necessity—in any career.

I have had the honor to work with many professionals like you, who, while mastering the skills and knowledge needed to excel in their fields, do not have a clear understanding of the natural sounds and rhythms of English. For example, a brilliant Chinese corporate executive for American Express had been repeatedly overlooked for promotion because his English pronunciation was unclear, and he was often misunderstood in meetings and on conference calls. After we worked with the *Perfecting Your English Pronunciation* method, he understood exactly which sounds were difficult for him and how to correct them—and was able to conduct meetings with ease. Shortly thereafter, he received the promotion he deserved.

I am a strong advocate of diversity in the workplace, and the last thing I want to do is to make all people "sound alike." Many clients have expressed the fear that, in working on accent modification, they will lose their sense of identity, since their speech is a reflection of who they are as individuals and as representatives of their own particular cultures. I completely understand this concern, and I would never advocate nor attempt a homogenization of a global business community. Rather, I am pursuing the opposite result: The goal of the *Perfecting Your English Pronunciation* method is not to reduce the appearance of ethnicity, but to offer individuals the option of speaking clearer Global English (or "Business English," that is, English without the idioms of native speakers). This showcases each person's unique identity and allows expertise to shine through.

I have coached thousands of clients from all over the world—from geographical areas and cultures as diverse as Asia (Japan, India, Korea, China, Hong Kong, Thailand, Singapore, Taiwan and Vietnam); South American (Venezuela, Argentina, Brazil, Chile, Peru, Colombia, Ecuador); Hispanic cultures, such as Puerto Rico, the Dominican Republic, and Mexico; Europe (France, Germany, Switzerland, Portugal, Spain, Italy, Greece, Netherlands, all countries in the British Isles, Russia, and other Eastern European countries, including Hungary, the Czech Republic, Poland, Romania, Albania, Estonia, Turkey, Armenia, Serbia, and Croatia); Middle Eastern countries, including Israel, Lebanon, United Arab Emirates, Egypt, Iraq, and Iran; and Africa (Nigeria, Kenya, Ghana, and South Africa) From this large cross section of students, I have identified the 14 difficult sounds and groups of sounds of English pronunciation for all nonnative speakers. And with *Perfecting Your English Pronunciation*, I have never seen the Cameron Method of Accent Modification® fail.

Part One introduces the physical placement of sound and the musculature used in articulation. Many other languages rely heavily on the back of the tongue to articulate sounds; by contrast, most sounds in English are formed at the front of the mouth, using the tip of the tongue and the musculature of the lips for consonant placement. You may have trouble with English pronunciation because of excessive tension in the back of your tongue, as well as lack of muscle development in the tip of your tongue and lips. The good news is that this problem is easily overcome by using the exercises described in Chapter One. Think of it as your mouth going to the gym for 10 minutes every day. These exercises are also demonstrated on the accompanying videos.

Also in Part One, we introduce the system of phonetics, the International Phonetic Alphabet, and provide an overview of the 48 sounds, or phonemes, of the English language.

Part Two forms the core of this book, with one chapter devoted to each of the 14 phonemes and groups of phonemes that you may find difficult to pronounce. Each sound's precise anatomical placement is described in the text, then demonstrated on the videos. You will need a hand mirror to check for the correct physical placement of sounds; a freestanding mirror is best, since it allows free use of your hands to practice the exercises. The text contains tricks to perfect sound placement, such as putting a finger to your lips to discourage excessive tightening of a vowel.

Audio recordings are provided to train your ears in the differentiation of difficult sounds, within words, phrases, and sentences. You have the option of recording your practice sessions within the app to compare them with those on the audio recordings.

A huge asset of this book is that it can serve as a mini pronunciation dictionary: Each chapter contains word lists—in all, 8,400 of the most commonly used and mispronounced words in English, grouped by sound pattern. New for this revised edition, all of these words have been recorded and can be practiced by following the word list recordings via the app.

Part Three of *Perfecting Your English Pronunciation* has the "goodies." It addresses the issues of stress, intonation, and operative vs. inoperative words, which collectively create the rhythm of English speech. I say "goodies," because this rhythm often seems to be the most elusive aspect for those struggling with English pronunciation. We focus on stress within words, as well as stress within sentences (also called intonation). Stress within words is often dictated by suffix patterns, which explains the shifting stress in the words *démonstrate, demónstrative,* and *demonstrátion.* The precise rules for syllable stress within words as determined by suffix patterns are explained. Operative and inoperative words are analyzed—those that carry the information in a sentence, as opposed to those that merely provide grammatical structure. Understanding this concept allows you to determine which words are stressed within phrases, clauses, and sentences.

In Part Four, instructions are provided on how to mark and score all your presentations for clearer pronunciation. Sample business presentations are marked for intonation and flagged for difficult sounds. Included are three case studies featuring clients of the Cameron Method®; these clients dramatically improved their pronunciation using this technique, and the case studies include "before" and "after" recordings of their presentations via the app.

Welcome to *Perfecting Your English Pronunciation.* Let's get started!

PART ONE

GETTING STARTED

ONE

Retraining the articulation muscles

The human body is a glorious, deeply complicated, and vastly explored phenomenon of nature. Most of us can appreciate this concept through the prism of poets and scientists alike. We speak of the "heart" to describe feelings and emotions that defy scientific explanation; we also (sometimes) listen to doctors who tell us to stop eating fast food if we want our hearts to continue pumping oxygen to all our cells. Poets speak of that which "takes our breath away"; scientists point out that smoking usually does. So we accept that both approaches to the body—mental/emotional health and systemic physical wellness—exist simultaneously and in perfect symmetry.

Why, then, do we not usually accept the fact that language—and the pronunciation of each individual language—is mostly a physical phenomenon, dictated by the dexterity of the articulating muscles that are used in forming speech? I believe this is because speech is a highly personal issue. Indeed, this viewpoint is supported by many idioms in English-speaking cultures: We talk of "having a voice," of "speaking up for ourselves," of "being rendered speechless" versus "shouting to the mountaintops"—all poetic descriptions of the mental and emotional state that predetermines our proclivity for expression.

But when Fred faced his Monday afternoon meeting (see page xix), the last thing on his mind was that, poetically speaking, he had a "lump in his throat" and that nervousness might leave him "tongue-tied." All he knew—or cared about—was that his thoughts were crystal clear and that his speech was not. It was almost, he thought, as he took a sip of water, cleared his throat, and began to speak, that he couldn't *get his mouth to*

3

work fast enough to catch up to the words that were coming out of it. Ironic, yes. But, physiologically speaking, this was exactly what was happening to Fred.

The articulators of speech

Obviously, Fred was upset. He knew he had made so much progress in speaking English—and that doing articulation muscle training felt like he would be "starting from scratch." So, in our session together, I used an analogy. "Suppose you were a marathon runner. You could run 26 miles in less than three hours. And you could sprint a mile in three and a half minutes flat. Your physical condition would be remarkable, and your domination in your field irrefutable, yes?" Fred nodded, and I continued, "Now, because your lower body muscles are in such great shape, I can therefore expect you to walk over to a set of barbells and chest press 300 pounds. Right?"

Fred understood the analogy, even though he was not a marathon runner and had never bench pressed in his life. Different physical disciplines determine different muscle structure. Theoretically, you may be able to squat press exceptionally well, but not excel at chest pressing. So it is with speech: Different languages use the articulation muscles differently. For example, the back of your tongue may be exponentially stronger than the tip of your tongue, based on how your native language utilizes the muscle.

We need to examine the physiology of speech in an objective way. The articulation muscles can be divided into the following categories: the jaw muscle group, the soft palate, the back of the tongue, the tip of the tongue, and the lips. Together, these produce physical speech. Therefore, to learn to pronounce Global English correctly, we have to study—and exercise—all of the articulators that facilitate clear diction.

Video exercises

The exercises on the accompanying app will retrain your articulation muscles in order to master clear Global English speech. Specifically, they focus on the jaw, the soft palate, the back of the tongue, the tip of the tongue, and the lips.

To retrain these muscles and to practice anatomical placement, you must work with a mirror; a freestanding mirror that frees your hands is best. You have to become accustomed to looking inside your mouth at your own articulation muscles, or else you will hinder your progress. For Fred, an inferior performance at an important meeting is far more uncomfortable than 10 minutes in front of a mirror. Some of the placement exercises may require you to feel inside your mouth with your little finger, since retraining the tongue muscle is often realized more readily through tactile placement than through ear training alone. To practice these exercises, first wash your hands, then position yourself in front of the mirror.

These exercises will help you strengthen the articulators in your mouth. Details of individual sound placement follow in later chapters.

The first major muscle that contributes to speech is the jaw muscle group. You may be familiar with the archetype of the "angry young man" that abounds in film—the guy with a clenched, locked jaw, mumbling speech, and finely chiseled bone structure. As enviable as the bone structure might be, the locked jaw is problematic; clear Global English speech requires space in the mouth, and a relaxed jaw makes articulation easier.

Exercises for the jaw

VIDEO

1

*Watch **Video Articulation Exercises 1** before attempting the following exercises.* It is important that you perform the retraining exercises correctly. After watching, read the instructions for the jaw exercises, then begin practicing.

1. Release your jaw. Feel it drop open as you part your lips and breathe through your mouth. Feel your tongue resting on the floor of your mouth, with the tip of your tongue resting against your lower teeth, and the back of your tongue down, away from the roof of your mouth.*

---

*This is the base position for the tongue in clear Global English. Practicing this tongue position reduces tongue tension.

Feel how much easier it is to take deep breaths with your jaw re-laxed and your tongue resting on the floor of your mouth than it is with your tongue "stuck" to the roof of your mouth and your jaw clenched.

Go back and forth between these two placements—jaw relaxed and breathing through your mouth, then jaw clenched and breathing through your nose. Feel the difference in overall tension between the two.

2. Place your fingers on your jaw muscle. Grit your teeth together and chew. Find the center of your jaw muscle, the point of greatest tension. Now relax your jaw and press the knuckles of your index fingers against the tension point, as hard as you can tolerate. This may feel uncomfort-able, since you are breaking up residual tension in the jaw muscle. Hold this position for 15 seconds.

3. Release your hands and feel your jaw drop farther. Take hold of your jaw with both hands and gently pull it downward—but not as far as it can go, pulling the bones out of their joints. You should develop a relaxation in your jaw muscle that allows for a full opening, without joint displacement.

4. Continue moving your jaw up and down, adding sound. Make sure that you are moving your jaw with your hands, not letting your jaw move by itself (that is, not letting your hands "go along for the ride").

5. Press your knuckles against your jaw muscle once again. Practice until you can hold this position for 60 seconds.

6. Shake your jaw out, again adding sound.

These exercises will release your clenched jaw and begin to remedy mum-bled speech.

Exercises for the soft palate

VIDEO

2

*Watch **Video Articulation Exercises 2** before attempting the following exer-cises.* It is important that you perform the retraining exercises correctly. After watching, read the instructions for the soft palate exercises, then begin practicing.

1. Take out your mirror and look inside your mouth. Notice your tongue lying flat on the floor of the mouth, the tip of the tongue resting against your bottom teeth. Imagine that there is superglue on the tip of your tongue. Glue, or anchor, the tip of your tongue to your lower teeth. Try to yawn, and watch the back of your throat as the soft palate is engaged. You should see—and feel—a raise and stretching at the back of the throat.
2. Now, form a k sound, then inhale. Look inside your mouth in the mirror. For a full palatal stretch, your soft palate should rise and the back of your tongue should drop down.
3. Practice inhaling and exhaling on a k sound, watching for sharp articulation of the soft palate.
4. With your index finger, hold the front and middle of your tongue in the anchored position (remember the superglue image). Voice a ng-a, ng-a, ng-a sound. Again, watch for agility in the soft palate. (Any tendency to say ng-ga is evidence of tightness in the palate or the back of the tongue.) Repeat this at an increasingly more rapid speed.
5. Practice ng-a on different riffs of rhythm and pitch.

Exercises for the back of the tongue

VIDEO

3

*Watch **Video Articulation Exercises 3** before attempting the following exercises.* It is important that you perform the retraining exercises correctly. After watching, read the instructions for the back of the tongue exercises, then begin practicing.

We mentioned earlier how strong the back of your tongue probably is. But all that strength requires a lot of stretching to keep the muscle loose and flexible.

1. Place the tip of your tongue behind your lower teeth. Bulge the back of your tongue forward, stretching it as far as comfort permits. Check in the mirror, making sure that your jaw does not move too.
2. Repeat this motion, adding sound. Notice how much your jaw may tend to move now. With one hand, hold your jaw still while you repeat the exercise.

3. Increase the speed of the exercise, as you maintain the stretch in your tongue.

Exercises for the tip of the tongue

VIDEO

4

*Watch **Video Articulation Exercises 4** before attempting the following exercises.* It is important that you perform the retraining exercises correctly. After watching, read the instructions for the tip of the tongue exercises, then begin practicing.

Here come the figurative "chest presses" I mentioned to Fred earlier: strengthening the weaker tongue tip.

1. To focus the tip of your tongue for precision with alveolar consonants (see pages 15–16), point the tip of your tongue toward your little finger. Watching in the mirror, make sure that you do not tighten your jaw or lips.
2. Place your little finger underneath the tip of your tongue and push it up, while resisting with your tongue. Do not use the strength of the back of your tongue to compensate for weakness in the front; this is essentially an isometric exercise for the tip of your tongue. Hold for at least 10 seconds.
3. Relax. Then repeat, pointing your tongue and then pushing up for another 10 seconds.
4. Now let's bring in the artillery. Take a toothpick, and place it against the back of your upper front teeth. Slide it gently upward against your upper teeth, until it touches the gum. Just behind where your gum meets your upper teeth, you'll feel a small bony bump—this is the alveolar ridge. (If the toothpick is pointed, be careful not to jab the gum.) The alveolar consonants (t, d, n, and l) are produced by touching the alveolar ridge with the tip of your tongue. The only sound in English that is made with the tongue touching the toothpick is the *th* sound. Practice making a t sound against the alveolar ridge, making sure that your tongue does not touch the toothpick.
5. Pause the video. With the toothpick still in place, make a t sound in time with the ticking of the second hand of a clock, for one minute. Be sure that the t sounds are crisp and made against the alveolar ridge.

Exercises for the lips

VIDEO

5

*Watch **Video Articulation Exercises 5** before attempting the following exercises.* It is important that you perform the retraining exercises correctly. After watching, read the instructions for the lip exercises, then begin practicing.

1. Pop your lips forward, using the musculature at the center of both the upper and lower lips. Pause the video. Make a popping p sound in time with the ticking of the second hand of a clock, for one minute.
2. Flutter out your lips by relaxing and blowing air lightly through them. Be careful to leave your jaw relaxed, and make sure your tongue is in the base position, at the bottom of your mouth with the tip behind your lower teeth. Hold your hand six inches from your mouth. Aim your breath so that you feel it touching the palm of your hand.
3. Now, "throw a dart" in slow motion, fluttering out your lips. Make sure that you do this all in one breath.
4. Repeat this exercise.

Stop plosive consonants

VIDEO

6

*Watch **Video Articulation Exercises 6** before attempting the following exercises.* It is important that you perform the retraining exercises correctly. After watching, read the instructions for the articulation exercises, then begin practicing.

These exercises promote strength and focus in the tip of the tongue. The last two—k and g—also promote flexibility and dexterity of the soft palate and relaxation in the back of the tongue.

1. Practice individual stop plosive consonants as follows.
   a. puh-puh-puh, puh-puh-puh, puh-puh-puh, PAH
   b. buh-buh-buh, buh-buh-buh, bub-buh-buh, BAH
   c. tuh-tuh-tuh, tuh-tuh-tuh, tuh-tuh-tuh, TAH
   d. duh-duh-duh, duh-duh-duh, duh-duh-duh, DAH
   e. kuh-kuh-kuh, kuh-kuh-kuh, kuh-kuh-kuh, KAH
   f. guh-guh-guh, guh-guh-guh, guh-guh-guh, GAH

2. Altogether:
   puh puh PAH, buh buh BAH, tuh tuh TAH,
   duh duh DAH, kuh kuh KAH, guh guh GAH

   Try it again, but this time, all in one breath. Make sure that your jaw remains perfectly still throughout the exercise.

3. For the grand finale, do the exercise forward and backward:
   puh puh PAH, buh buh BAH, tuh tuh TAH, duh duh DAH,
   kuh kuh KAH, guh guh GAH, guh guh GAH, kuh kuh KAH,
   duh duh DAH, tuh tuh TAH, buh buh BAH, puh puh PAH

Congratulations! Your mouth has just completed a full workout at the speech gym.

TWO

The International Phonetic Alphabet

As we saw in the Introduction, the words *stop, go,* and *other* are all spelled with the letter *o,* but they have three different vowel *sounds.* Over the centuries, English has adopted so many words from other languages that its spelling patterns are confusing at best, and at worst they seem arbitrary.

In the late 19th century, a group of British and French linguists invented the International Phonetic Alphabet (IPA), a system that uniquely identifies all of the sounds, or phonemes, used in human languages. Each sound is represented by a single symbol, and conversely, each symbol represents a single sound. The linguists advocated that English spelling be reformed, using a phonetic alphabet to represent the exact pronunciation of words. Unfortunately for us, they lost the battle. Fortunately, they devised a phonetic system by which we can precisely identify pronunciation.

The English language uses 48 sounds: 24 consonants and 24 vowels (including 12 pure vowels, 10 diphthongs, and two triphthongs). A **consonant** is a sound in which the voice, or breath stream, is interrupted or impeded during production. Consonants can be either voiced or voiceless; if the vocal folds vibrate during production, the consonant is voiced, and if they do not vibrate, the consonant is voiceless. All consonants are formed by using two of seven articulators (the lips, the tip of the tongue, the middle of the tongue, the back of the tongue, the alveolar ridge, the hard palate, and the soft palate) either touching or in proximity to each other.

A **vowel**, by contrast, is an uninterrupted voiced sound. For all vowel sounds (with the exception of the vowels, diphthongs, and triphthongs of *r*), the tongue rests on the floor of the mouth, with its tip resting against the lower teeth, and the arch in the tongue determines the phoneme produced.

By now, you have watched the Video Articulation Exercises and mastered the daily warm-up. Let's move now to the specific articulator placement for consonant and vowel sounds.

Introduction to the consonant sounds

Consonants can be divided into six major categories: stop plosives, nasals, the lateral, fricatives, glides, and affricates. Each of these is named for the way in which the breath stream, or voice, is impeded or interrupted while producing the sound.

Let's review the physiology of the articulators (see the Video Articulation Exercises and the illustration on page 20). Just behind the upper teeth, where the gums begin, you'll feel a small bony bump. This is called the **alveolar ridge**. Proceeding toward the back, there is the bony roof of the mouth, also known as the **hard palate**. Behind this is a soft fleshy area called the **soft palate**. We explored this in the initial retraining articulation exercises; it is the area of the mouth engaged when yawning and can be most fully sensed when forming a k, g, or ng sound. The **tongue** can be divided into three distinct areas: the back, the middle, and the tip. Other consonant articulators include the **lips** and, less frequently, the **upper teeth**.

As mentioned above, consonants can be either voiceless or voiced. Place your hand on your larynx, or voice box, and say the following sounds: p, then b. Say only the consonant sound—do not add a vowel, as in *puh*. Notice that your vocal folds are not engaged—there is no vibration—for the p sound, but they are engaged for the b. These partner sounds are called **cognate pairs**: Both consonants are produced with the same articulators in the same position, but one of the consonants is voiceless and the other voiced.

Don't worry: While all this information seems very technical, most consonant sounds are intuitively pronounced correctly by English for

Speakers of Other Languages (ESOL) students. Those that may be mispronounced are covered in detail in Part Two (The difficult sounds of English).

The consonants

Most consonants may occur in initial, medial, and final positions in words. **Initial position** is at the beginning of a word, **medial position** is in the middle of a word, and **final position** is at the end of a word. All of these positions are demonstrated in the word examples below; exceptions are noted for certain consonants.

We are now entering the world of phonetics. From now on, we will use the IPA symbol for each sound, rather than the alphabet spelling. IPA symbols are set in sans serif type (for example, b, d, g or *b, d, g*), while spelled words are set in serif type (for example, base, dance, go or *base, dance, go*).

Stop plosives

The breath stream is "stopped," then "exploded" to produce a **stop plosive**. English has six stop plosives.

VOICED PLOSIVE	EXAMPLE WORDS	VOICELESS PLOSIVE	EXAMPLE WORDS
b	base, suburban, cab	p	pay, repeat, stop
d	dance, redeem, need	t	time, intense, past
g	go, regret, flag	k	keep, decrease, desk

Nasals

The sound is released through the nose to produce a **nasal**. English has only three sounds that are nasal. All three are voiced.

VOICED NASAL	EXAMPLE WORDS
m	men, remember, phoneme
n	news, renew, plan
ŋ (ng)	kingdom, thank

Note that ŋ is never used in initial position.

Lateral

The **lateral** is produced laterally, over the sides of the tongue. The tip of the tongue remains in contact with the alveolar ridge, and the sound is always voiced. English has only one lateral.

VOICED LATERAL	EXAMPLE WORDS
l	last, billing, final

Fricatives

A **fricative** is named for the friction created by forcing the breath stream or voice between two articulators. English has nine fricatives.

VOICED FRICATIVE	EXAMPLE WORDS	VOICELESS FRICATIVE	EXAMPLE WORDS
v	victory, invite, save	f	free, affirm, off
ð (th)	this, other, soothe	θ (th)	think, method, math
z	zoo, resume, please	s	see, receive, miss
ʒ (zh)	genre, pleasure, beige	ʃ (sh)	shout, worship, wish
		h	hotel, behind

Note that h is never used in final position.

Glides

The articulators move from one position to another to produce a **glide**. Glides are voiced and are always followed by a vowel sound. English has three glides.

VOICED GLIDE	EXAMPLE WORDS
w	wish, rewind
j (y or *liquid* u)	yesterday, beyond, music
r (*consonant* r)	right, bereft

Note that none of these three consonant sounds, w, j, and r, is ever used in final position.

Affricates

An **affricate** is a combination of a stop plosive and a fricative, blended seamlessly into a single phoneme. English has two affricates.

VOICED AFFRICATE	EXAMPLE WORDS	VOICELESS AFFRICATE	EXAMPLE WORDS
ʤ (j or g)	jazz, adjust, age	ʧ (ch)	cheer, achieve, touch

Consonant overview

VOICED CONSONANT	VOICELESS CONSONANT	PLACEMENT AND DESCRIPTION

Stop plosives

b	p	Bilabial (using both lips). The lips come together, then pop apart.
d	t	Alveolar (using the gum ridge behind the upper teeth). The tip of the tongue pops off the alveolar ridge.
g	k	Velar (using the soft palate). The back of the tongue touches the soft palate, then they pop apart.

Nasals

m		Bilabial. The lips come together, the soft palate is lowered, and the sound is released through the nose.
n		Alveolar. The tip of the tongue touches the alveolar ridge, the soft palate is lowered, and the sound is released through the nose.
ŋ		Velar. The back of the tongue touches the soft palate, which is lowered, and the sound is released through the nose.

Continued

Consonant overview (*continued*)

VOICED CONSONANT	VOICELESS CONSONANT	PLACEMENT AND DESCRIPTION
Lateral		
l		Alveolar. The tip of the tongue contacts the alveolar ridge.
Fricatives		
v	f	Labiodental (using the lower lip and the upper teeth). The lower lip contacts the bottom of the upper teeth.
ð	θ	Dental (using the tip of the tongue and the the upper teeth). The tip of the tongue contacts the bottom of the upper teeth.
z	s	Alveolar. The tip of the tongue is in proximity to the alveolar ridge.
ʒ	ʃ	Alveolar. The front of the tongue is in proximity to the alveolar ridge, and the lips are slightly rounded.
h		Glottal (using the space between the vocal folds). The sound is released through relaxed vocal folds.
Glides		
w		Bilabial. The lips come together and are rounded.
j		Lingual-palatal (using the middle of the tongue and the hard palate). The tip of the tongue is behind the lower teeth, and the middle of the tongue is arched toward the hard palate.
r		Alveolar. The tongue is raised toward the alveolar ridge.
Affricates		
dʒ	tʃ	Alveolar. The tip of the tongue contacts the alveolar ridge, then is pulled back.

Introduction to the vowel sounds

Vowels are uninterrupted, or unimpeded, voiced sounds. Except for the vowels, diphthongs, and triphthongs of *r*, all vowels are made with the tip of the tongue resting against the lower teeth. It is the arch in the front, middle, or back of the tongue that determines the phoneme. *This is important, since most ESOL students have tension in the back of the tongue that causes the tongue muscle to retract (pull back) during vowel articulation.*

Vowels can be divided into three categories: pure vowels, diphthongs, and triphthongs. In the production of a **pure vowel**, the arch in the tongue is fixed throughout the duration of the sound. A **diphthong** is a blend of two pure vowels sounded together as one. A **triphthong** is three vowels sounds blended together as one.

The pure vowel sounds can be categorized as front, middle, and back, named for the arch in the tongue. For a **front vowel**, the front of the tongue is arched; for a **middle vowel**, the middle of the tongue is arched; and for a **back vowel**, the back of the tongue is arched (with the exception of the vowel ɑ, for which the back of the tongue is flat).

The differences between some of these sounds may seem minimal at first, but we will use a tactile approach, so that you can feel each vowel's placement while you simultaneously train your ear. Don't worry if some vowels seem difficult to make at this point. This chapter is intended to be an introduction to the physical placement of vowels according to the arch in the tongue; Part Two explores each of the problematic vowel phonemes in detail, and all the vowel positions are demonstrated in the videos in the accompanying app.

We are now going to start transcribing entire words using the IPA. Notice how logical the pronunciation seems when viewed through the prism of phonetics. *Note:* When a word contains two or more syllables, one syllable will be stressed more than the others. This syllable is said to carry primary stress and is preceded by the symbol '.

The vowels

English has 12 pure vowels, as shown in the pure vowel overview chart on page 18.

Once you have learned the pure vowels, combining two or three vowels to form a diphthong or triphthong should be easy ('izi). English has 10 diphthongs and two triphthongs, as shown in the charts on page 19.

Pure vowel overview

IPA	SPELLING PATTERNS	EXAMPLE WORDS

Front vowels

i	e, ea, ee, ei, ey, ie, y	be, heat, see, receive, key, chief, happy bi, hit, si, rɪ'siv, ki, ʧif, 'hæpi
ɪ	i, y (*except in final position*)	it, hit, miss, since, myth ɪt, hɪt, mɪs, sɪns, mɪθ
e	e, ea	jet, mess, dread, head ʤet, mes, dred, hed
æ	a	ask, man, thanks, jazz æsk, mæn, θæŋks, ʤæz

Middle vowels

ɝ	ear, er, ir, or, ur	rehearsal, person, stir, worst, purpose rɪ'hɝsəl, 'pɝsən, stɝ, wɝst, 'pɝpəs
ɚ	er, or (*unstressed syllables*)	singer, mother, actor, comfort 'sɪŋɚ, 'mʌðɚ, 'æktɚ, 'kʌmfɚt
ə	schwa (*vowel reduction; see pages 235–237*)	the, affront, introduction, dependent ðə, ə'frʌnt, ɪntrə'dʌkʃən, dɪ'pendənt
ʌ	o, u	other, love, cup, judge, must 'ʌðɚ, lʌv, kʌp, ʤʌʤ, mʌst

Back vowels

u	ew, o, oe, oo, u, ue	stew, who, shoe, food, flu, blue stu, hu, ʃu, fud, flu, blu
ʊ	o, oo, ou, u	woman, good, book, should, push 'wʊmən, gʊd, bʊk, ʃʊd, pʊʃ
ɔ	a(l), au, aw, oad, ough	all, August, law, broad, thought ɔl, 'ɔgəst, lɔ, brɔd, θɔt
ɑ	a, o (*see Chapter Sixteen*)	father, doctor, stop, body 'faðɚ, 'dɑktɚ, stɑp, 'bɑdi

Diphthong overview

IPA	SPELLING PATTERNS	EXAMPLE WORDS
eɪ̆	a, ai, ay, ei, ey	date, grain, day, freight, weigh, they deɪ̆t, greɪ̆n, deɪ̆, freɪ̆t, weɪ̆, ðeɪ̆
aɪ̆	i, y	time, might, fright, I, sigh, fly taɪ̆m, maɪ̆t, fraɪ̆t, aɪ̆, saɪ̆, flaɪ̆
ɔɪ̆	oi, oy	boil, oil, joy, boy, annoy bɔɪ̆l, ɔɪ̆l, dʒɔɪ̆, bɔɪ̆, ə'nɔɪ̆
oʊ̆	o, oa, ow	go, home, phone, ago, load, know goʊ̆, hoʊ̆m, foʊ̆n, ə'goʊ̆, loʊ̆d, noʊ̆
aʊ̆	ou, ow	about, out, how, now, downtown ə'baʊ̆t, aʊ̆t, haʊ̆, naʊ̆, 'daʊ̆ntaʊ̆n

Diphthongs of *r*

IPA	SPELLING PATTERNS	EXAMPLE WORDS
ɪɚ	ear, eer, ere	clear, fear, steer, cheer, mere klɪɚ, fɪɚ, stɪɚ, tʃɪɚ, mɪɚ
eɚ	air, are	hair, fair, stairs, dare, aware heɚ, feɚ, steɚz, deɚ, ə'weɚ
ʊɚ	oor, our, ure	poor, tour, yours, cure, sure pʊɚ, tʊɚ, jʊɚz, kjʊɚ, ʃʊɚ
ɔɚ	oor, or, ore, our	door, floor, or, more, four, pour dɔɚ, flɔɚ, ɔɚ, mɔɚ, fɔɚ, pɔɚ
ɑɚ	ar	dark, star, far, car, park, stark dɑɚk, stɑɚ, fɑɚ, kɑɚ, pɑɚk, stɑɚk

Triphthong overview

IPA	SPELLING PATTERNS	EXAMPLE WORDS
aɪ̆ɚ	ire, yer	fire, retire, tired, buyer, flyer faɪ̆ɚ, rɪ'taɪ̆ɚ, taɪ̆ɚd, baɪ̆ɚ, flaɪ̆ɚ
aʊ̆ɚ	our, ower	our, hour, scour, power, tower aʊ̆ɚ, aʊ̆ɚ, skaʊ̆ɚ, paʊ̆ɚ, taʊ̆ɚ

Now that you have mastered the articulation retraining exercises and understand how the International Phonetic Alphabet is used to indicate the sounds of English, we can turn to the 14 difficult sounds and groups of sounds of English placement. But first, let's take a look at where the vowel sounds are physically produced in the mouth. We'll use a drawing of Fred's head to map vowel placement.

Fred's head says . . .

This chart of the 12 pure vowels of English shows the arch in the tongue for front, middle, and back vowels. For all vowels except ɝ and ɚ, the tip of the tongue is resting against the lower teeth.

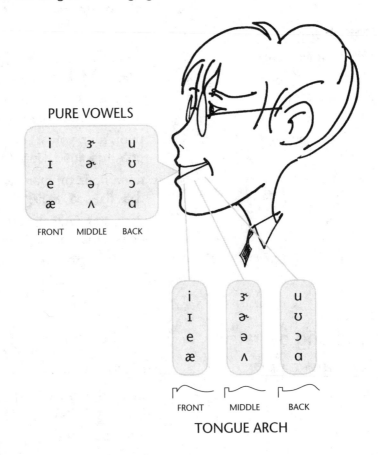

PURE VOWELS

i	ɝ	u
I	ɚ	ʊ
e	ə	ɔ
æ	ʌ	ɑ

FRONT   MIDDLE   BACK

i	ɝ	u
I	ɚ	ʊ
e	ə	ɔ
æ	ʌ	ɑ

FRONT   MIDDLE   BACK

TONGUE ARCH

PART TWO

THE DIFFICULT SOUNDS OF ENGLISH

THREE

The consonant *th* (θ/ð)

Fred was being considered for a new position in his marketing firm: a job that would require frequent oral presentations in English. Fred's boss began to call on him in meetings, and Fred knew that his performance was under scrutiny. Public speaking in English ignited Fred's fears. His mouth would become dry, and he felt his breath grow short and shallow. Fred decided to confide in a colleague. After an especially difficult meeting, he pulled Margaret aside, and told her, in confidence, "I have trouble breeding." Margaret was confused . . .

The *th* sound defined

The *th* sound can be either voiceless (as in the word *thin*) or voiced (as in *then*). The placement is the same, but in the voiceless sound, the vocal folds do not vibrate, and in the voiced sound, they do. These sounds are represented by the phonetic symbols θ (voiceless *th,* as in *thin*) and ð (voiced *th,* as in *then*). Nonnative speakers of English often mispronounce *th* in the following ways: Voiceless *th* (θ) is usually replaced by the consonant t (as in *tin*), and voiced *th* (ð) is usually replaced by d (as in *den*). This is an understandable mistake, since t and d are found in nearly all languages, and the *th* sounds occur almost exclusively in English.

The sounds θ/ð are made very close to t/d, but with a definite difference in tongue placement. For both the t and d consonants, the tip of the tongue touches the alveolar ridge, then flicks off it. When producing a t, the vocal folds do not vibrate; when forming a d, they do. (You may want to refer to the tip of the tongue exercises in Chapter One. Be sure that you are forming t and d off the alveolar ridge, not against the back of your teeth.) θ/ð, on the other hand, are formed with the tip of your tongue touching the bottom of your upper teeth.

Step 1: Feeling the placement of θ/ð

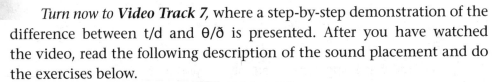

VIDEO
7

Turn now to **Video Track 7,** where a step-by-step demonstration of the difference between t/d and θ/ð is presented. After you have watched the video, read the following description of the sound placement and do the exercises below.

Take out your mirror. Begin by saying the t sound, since you already pronounce this sound correctly. Say the word *tin* several times. Looking in the mirror, begin to become aware of your tongue's placement. Notice that the tip of your tongue touches the alveolar ridge, then flicks quickly off it. Now, lightly place the tip of your tongue against the bottom of your upper teeth. It is not necessary to use the whole front of your tongue. This is the placement for voiceless *th*, θ, as in *thin*. Go back and forth between these two placements: t . . . θ . . . t . . . θ.

Put your fingers against your larynx and say d. Notice that your vocal folds are vibrating, and that the tip of your tongue touches the alveolar ridge, then flicks quickly off it. Now, place the tip of your tongue against the bottom of your upper teeth and allow your vocal folds to vibrate. This is voiced *th*, ð, as in *then*. Alternate between these two placements: d . . . ð . . . d . . . ð.

Return now to **Video Track 7.** Practice the difference in placement between the consonants t/d and θ/ð.

Step 2: Hearing the placement of θ/ð

Using your mirror, look closely inside your mouth. Move your tongue back and forth between the placements of these two pairs of words: *tin, thin, tin, thin* and *den, then, den, then.* (Of course, the tip of your tongue will touch the alveolar ridge for the final consonant n.)

Watch in the mirror as you pronounce the pairs of words in the following list. Listen to the consonant sound changes as well, so that you can train your ear to hear the distinction, as well as feel the physiological difference in placement.

t/d	θ/ð
team	theme
tank	thank
tick	thick
tie	thigh
torn	thorn
trash	thrash
tread	thread
tree	three
trust	thrust
tug	thug
dare	there
day	they
dough	though
doze	those
dense	thence

AUDIO

3.1

*Turn now to **Audio Track 3.1**, which features the sound adjustments between t/d and θ/ð. Repeat the pairs of words, while comparing your pronunciation with that on the recording.

Record your own pronunciation, and compare it to the recording. Repeat this exercise until you feel ready to proceed to the next step.

Step 3: Applying the placement of θ/ð

Following are lists of common English words that contain the *th* sounds. You can practice these sounds by checking your pronunciation against the word list recordings. After you have mastered the sounds, advance to the phrases. Then move on to the sentences.

AUDIO
3.2

INITIAL ð (VOICED *th*)

that	thence	this
the	there	those
their	therefore	though
them	these	thus
then	they	

MEDIAL ð (VOICED *th*)

another	heathen	slather
blather	heather	slither
bother	hither	smother
brethren	lather	southern
brother	leather	swarthy
clothing	logarithm	together
either	mother	weather
father	neither	whether
fathom	northern	wither
feather	other	within
farther	rather	without
further	rhythm	
gather	scathing	

FINAL ð (VOICED *th*)

bathe	mouth (*verb*)	soothe
blithe	scythe	teethe
breathe	seethe	tithe
lithe	sheathe	with
loath	smooth	

INITIAL θ (VOICELESS *th*)

thank	theory	thick
thatch	therapy	thicket
theater	thermometer	thief
theft	thermos	thigh
theme	thermostat	thimble
theocracy	thesaurus	thin
theology	thesis	thing ►

◄ think   thrash   throttle
third   threat   through
thirst   thread   throughout
thirteen   three   throw
thirty   thresh   thrust
thistle   threshold   thud
thong   thrifty   thug
thorax   thrill   thumb
thorn   thrive   thump
thorough   throat   thunder
thought   throb   Thursday
thousand   throne   thwart
thrall   throng   thyroid

MEDIAL θ (VOICELESS *th*)

aesthetic   brothel   lithography
amethyst   catharsis   marathon
anathema   cathedral   mathematics
anesthesia   catheter   menthol
anthem   catholic   misanthrope
anthology   decathlon   Neanderthal
anthrax   diphtheria   ophthalmology
anthropology   diphthong   orthodox
anthropomorphic empathy   orthography
antipathy   enthrall   orthopedic
antithesis   enthusiasm   osteopathy
anything   ethereal   parenthesis
apathy   ethic   pathetic
apothecary   ethnic   pithy
arthritis   euthanasia   plethora
arithmetic   gothic   ruthless
atheism   hypothesize   something
athlete   isthmus   stethoscope
authentic   kinesthetic   sympathy
author   lecithin   synthesis
authority   lethal   synthetic
birthday   lethargic   urethra

FINAL θ (VOICELESS *th*)

ba<u>th</u>	fourteen<u>th</u>*	seven<u>th</u>*
bene
a<u>th</u>	four<u>th</u>*	shea<u>th</u>
ber<u>th</u>	fro<u>th</u>	six<u>th</u>*
bir<u>th</u>	gir<u>th</u>	slo<u>th</u>
boo<u>th</u>	grow<u>th</u>	sou<u>th</u>
bo<u>th</u>	hear<u>th</u>	steal<u>th</u>
bread<u>th</u>	ha<u>th</u>	streng<u>th</u>
brea<u>th</u>	heal<u>th</u>	tee<u>th</u>
bro<u>th</u>	leng<u>th</u>	ten<u>th</u>*
clo<u>th</u>	mir<u>th</u>	tru<u>th</u>
dea<u>th</u>	monoli<u>th</u>	twelf<u>th</u>*
dear<u>th</u>	mo<u>th</u>	twentie<u>th</u>*
dep<u>th</u>	mou<u>th</u> (*noun*)	uncou<u>th</u>
ear<u>th</u>	my<u>th</u>	wid<u>th</u>
eigh<u>th</u>*	nin<u>th</u>*	wor<u>th</u>
fifteen<u>th</u>*	nor<u>th</u>	wrea<u>th</u>
fif<u>th</u>*	oa<u>th</u>	you<u>th</u>
fil<u>th</u>	pa<u>th</u>	
for<u>th</u>	Sabba<u>th</u>	

Phrases: θ/ð

AUDIO

3.3

  Listen to the recording of the following phrases, then read the phrases aloud. Concentrate on correctly pronouncing the θ/ð sounds, which are marked phonetically.

  θ   ð
1 thanks ano<u>th</u>er

  θ θ
2 pa<u>th</u>etic <u>th</u>oughts

  θ   ð
3 ru<u>th</u>less fa<u>th</u>er

---

*All cardinal numbers except *one, two,* and *three* can be changed to ordinal numbers by adding θ at the end.

      ð   θ
4 bro<u>th</u>er <u>th</u>inks

   θ   ð
5 <u>th</u>ousands ga<u>th</u>ered

     ð   θ
6 sou<u>th</u>ern pa<u>th</u>

   ð   θ
7 <u>th</u>eir ca<u>th</u>arsis

   ð   θ
8 <u>th</u>at a<u>th</u>lete

       θ   ð
9 empa<u>th</u>etic mo<u>th</u>er

     ð   θ
10 soo<u>th</u>ing my<u>th</u>

    θ   ð
12 syn<u>th</u>etic lea<u>th</u>er

    ð   θ
12 ano<u>th</u>er au<u>th</u>or

    ð   θ
13 <u>th</u>ose <u>th</u>eories

     θ   ð
14 any<u>th</u>ing sca<u>th</u>ing

   θ   ð
15 a<u>th</u>letic clo<u>th</u>ing

    ð   θ
16 ra<u>th</u>er <u>th</u>ick

    ð   θ
17 ano<u>th</u>er bir<u>th</u>day

   ð   θ
18 <u>th</u>is <u>Th</u>ursday

    ð   θ
19 smo<u>th</u>ering tru<u>th</u>

   θ ð
20 wor<u>th</u> ga<u>th</u>ering

Sentences: θ/ð

AUDIO
3.4

Listen to the recording of the following sentences, then read the sentences aloud. Concentrate on correctly pronouncing the θ/ð sounds, which are marked phonetically.

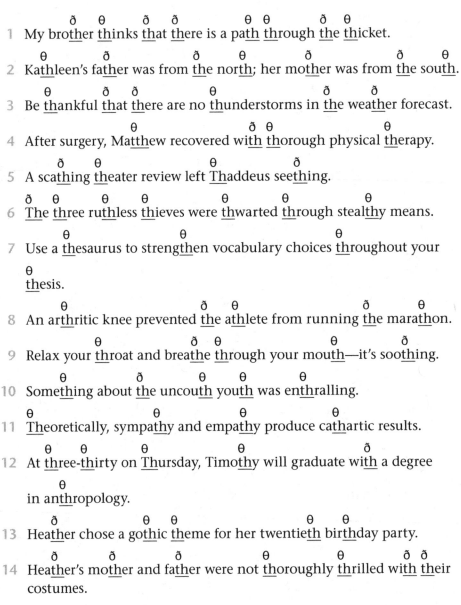

        ð   θ   ð   ð   θ θ   ð θ

1 My brother thinks that there is a path through the thicket.

       θ   ð   ð   θ   ð   ð   θ

2 Kathleen's father was from the north; her mother was from the south.

      θ   ð ð   θ   ð   ð

3 Be thankful that there are no thunderstorms in the weather forecast.

                    θ   ð θ   θ

4 After surgery, Matthew recovered with thorough physical therapy.

    ð   θ   θ   ð

5 A scathing theater review left Thaddeus seething.

  ð θ   θ   θ   θ   θ   θ

6 The three ruthless thieves were thwarted through stealthy means.

       θ   θ   θ

7 Use a thesaurus to strengthen vocabulary choices throughout your

  θ

thesis.

       θ   ð θ   ð   θ

8 An arthritic knee prevented the athlete from running the marathon.

        θ   ð θ   θ   ð

9 Relax your throat and breathe through your mouth—it's soothing.

     θ   ð   θ   θ   θ

10 Something about the uncouth youth was enthralling.

  θ   θ   θ   θ

11 Theoretically, sympathy and empathy produce cathartic results.

    θ   θ   θ   θ   ð

12 At three-thirty on Thursday, Timothy will graduate with a degree

       θ

in anthropology.

  ð   θ θ   θ   θ

13 Heather chose a gothic theme for her twentieth birthday party.

  ð   ð   ð   θ   θ   ð ð

14 Heather's mother and father were not thoroughly thrilled with their

costumes.

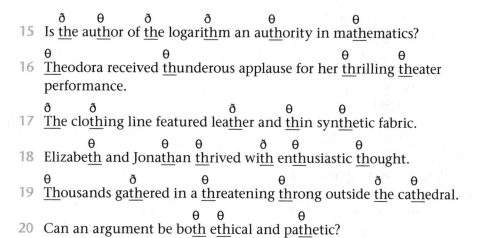

      ð   θ   ð   ð   θ   θ

15 Is the author of the logarithm an authority in mathematics?

    θ   θ   θ   θ

16 Theodora received thunderous applause for her thrilling theater performance.

   ð   ð   ð   θ   θ

17 The clothing line featured leather and thin synthetic fabric.

      θ   θ   θ   ð θ   θ

18 Elizabeth and Jonathan thrived with enthusiastic thought.

  θ   ð   θ   θ   ð θ

19 Thousands gathered in a threatening throng outside the cathedral.

                 θ θ   θ

20 Can an argument be both ethical and pathetic?

Phrases: θ/ð vs. *t/d*

AUDIO 3.5

Listen to the recording of the following phrases, then read the phrases aloud. Concentrate on distinguishing between the θ/ð and t/d sounds, which are marked phonetically.

  t   θ   θ

1 Tiny thin thief

     θ   t   d   t

2 enthusiastic dream team

  t   θ   d

3 ten healthy dinners

  t   t   θ   θ

4 trusting thorough therapy

  ð   θ   d   θ d

5 the fourth and fifth days

  θ   ð   t

6 thrilling weather alert

  t θ   t

7 truthful arguments

    ð   θ

8 leather cloth

  t   ð   ð

9 ten worthy brothers

```
         t        θ   d
10  teaching three days
         t            θ
11  turkey for Thanksgiving
         t   ð    ð
12  better than others
              θ       t
13  healthy vegetables
         θ        d d    t
14  three-year-old daughter
         d    d      ð
15  dependable fathers
         ð      d θ
16  further in depth
           t  t  θ
17  instinctive thinking
              t t       θ
18  argumentative youth
         t     θ      θ
19  twice in three months
         t      θ
20  torn on a thorn
```

Sentences: θ/ð vs. t/d

AUDIO

3.6

Listen to the recording of the following sentences, then read the sentences aloud. Concentrate on distinguishing between the θ/ð and t/d sounds, which are marked phonetically.

```
    ð     d  ð    t    t d t      ð   d      d  θ
1  The word farther pertains to distance; further describes depth.
    d   d       t t ð      d      d        ð
2  Do deer prefer to teethe on weeds or seeds—or neither?
       θ   d        θ      t      d  ð      t
3  Kathy, do you like Nathan's new tan-colored bathing suit?
       ð   d    t   t t    t       d     ð    ð      θ
4  In the department store, boots were sold in booths on the fourth
       d   θ
   and fifth floors.
```

ð   θ d θ   t   d t ð   ð

5 The unorthodox thesis was too wordy, but worthy nevertheless.

  d   t   d θ   d t   ð ð

6 Riding a roller coaster made three-year-old Tammy writhe with

  θ

enthusiasm.

ð   θ   d ð   t t d θ   t ð   d

7 The anesthesia allowed the patient to doze throughout the procedure.

 t   t   t   θ   ð   θ   d d   t t

8 Tom's team fought for fourth place in the healthy bread dough contest.

ð   d θ   t t ð d   θ   t ð   t

9 There's a birdbath next to the dense thicket on the nature trail.

ð θ   t   ð d t θ   d   ð θ   θ

10 The thorns tore the dainty thread in the thin cloth.

  θ   t   t   t θ   d   ð   t ð   θ d

11 I thought she taught three days, then took the fourth day off.

     t θ   d ð t   d ð   d   ð   θ

12 My cat, Theophilus, followed the trail of bird feathers down the path.

   t t   ð t θ   θ   ð   d t θ

13 Is it true that therapy can summon both soothing and truthful

θ   t

thoughts?

      θ t t   t d ð   θ   t   t t

14 Elizabeth trusts her wit and therefore is faithful to her instincts.

θ   t θ   θ   t t d ð   ð   t   d

15 Thrifty Matthew thinks tattered clothing is rather trendy.

ð   t   θ   t   t ð t θ   t

16 The paucity of thought inherent in that theological argument

      d ð   θ

challenged the faithful.

     θ   t   θ   θ   d d t d   θ

17 An authentic synthesis of various theories allowed deft design themes

t θ

to thrive.

   d d d ð d   θ   ð θ   dθ d   dθ   ð t

18 I dreaded the drive through the thick width and breadth of the trash

d

dump.

19 Theodora, thank you for your spectacularly thorough and thoughtful contribution!

20 You'll be thinner if dinners include healthy vegetables and no synthetic substances.

FOUR

The consonant *r*

The *r* sound defined

The consonant *r*, represented by the phonetic symbol r, is almost always mispronounced by nonnative speakers of English. Depending on your native language, you may pronounce r at the back of the throat, or you may trill it off the alveolar ridge. If your native language is Asian, you may pronounce r with tension in the back of your tongue, or the front of your tongue may be touching the roof of the mouth, much like an l.

Step 1: Feeling the placement of *r*

VIDEO

8

*Turn now to **Video Tracks 8A** and **8B**,* where a step-by-step demonstration of the placement of r is presented. After you have watched the video, read the following description of the sound placement and do the exercises below.

Take out your mirror. Let's examine the position of the tongue in forming the consonant r. Looking in the mirror, place the tip of your tongue against your lower teeth, with your tongue lying flat on the floor of your mouth. Now, arch the middle of your tongue toward the roof of your mouth and point the front of your tongue toward the alveolar ridge. Say r. You'll feel the sides of your tongue touching the inside of your upper teeth.

Again looking in the mirror, watch the movement of your tongue. The tip of your tongue begins against your lower teeth. Now, arch the middle of your tongue toward the hard palate, then lift the front of your tongue toward the alveolar ridge. This is the position for r. Make sure the tip of your tongue isn't touching anywhere inside your mouth.

The most difficult problem you will have with this new, unfamiliar placement is a tendency toward tongue retraction. Because the tip of your tongue isn't touching anywhere inside your mouth, the back of your tongue may tense and retract (pull backward) in order to feel "anchored." As demonstrated on the video, place your thumb under your jaw at the base of your tongue. Hold your thumb there firmly as you arch the middle of your tongue and lift the tip. This will prevent your tongue from retracting. You can anchor your tongue by feeling the sides of your tongue lightly touch the inside of the upper back teeth.

Return now to **Video Tracks 8A and 8B.** Practice the correct placement of the consonant r.

Step 2: Hearing the placement of *r*

Using the mirror, look closely inside your mouth. Move your tongue back and forth between the placements of these two pairs of words: *light, right, light, right.* (Of course, the tip of your tongue will touch the alveolar ridge for the final consonant t.) Notice that the tip of your tongue touches the alveolar ridge for l, but does not touch anywhere in your mouth for the consonant r.

Watch in the mirror as you pronounce the pairs of words in the list below. Listen to the consonant sound changes as well, so that you can train your ear to hear the distinction between l and r, as well as feel the physiological difference in placement.

l	r
lead	read (*both present-tense verbs*)
lie	rye
link	rink
load	road
led	red
lash	rash
low	row
loud	rowdy ►

l	r
◄	
lime	rhyme
blink	brink
class	crass
clear	rear
clam	ram
live (*adjective*)	drive
lip	drip

AUDIO
4.1

*Turn now to **Audio Track 4.1**,* which features the sound adjustments between l and r. Repeat the pairs of words, while comparing your pronunciation with that on the recording.

Record your own pronunciation, and compare it to the audio track. Repeat this exercise until you feel ready to proceed to the next step.

Step 3: Applying the placement of *r*

Following are lists of common English words that contain the *r* consonant. You can practice this sound by checking your pronunciation against the word list recordings. After you have mastered the sound, advance to the phrases. Then move on to the sentences.

AUDIO
4.2

INITIAL CONSONANT r*

brain	bring	cream
brake	British	create
branch	broad	credit
brave	Broadway	crew
bread	broke	crime
break	brother	crisis
breakfast	brought	critic
breath	brown	criticism
brick	brush	crop
bride	crack	cross
bridge	craft	crowd
brief	crash	crown
bright	crazy	cry	►

*As the initial sound or in a consonant combination at the beginning of a word.

INITIAL CONSONANT r* (*CONTINUED*)

◄ draft

draft	grand	price
drag	grant	pride
dramatic	grass	primary
draw	grave	primitive
dream	gray	print
dress	great	prior
drill	Greek	prison
drink	green	private
drive	greet	prize
drop	grew	procedure
drove	grin	process
drug	grip	procure
dry	gross	produce
fraction	ground	production
frame	group	productive
free	growth	professor
freedom	practice	profit
freeze	prayer	profound
freight	preceding	program
French	precious	progress
frequent	precision	project
fresh	prefer	prominent
Friday	prepare	promise
friend	present	promote
frightened	presentation	proof
from	preserve	propaganda
front	president	proper
frontier	press	property
frozen	pressure	proportion
fruit	prestige	propose
grab	presume	prospect
grace	pretty	protect
grade	prevent	protein
graduate	prevention	protest
grain	previous	proud ►

*As the initial sound or in a consonant combination at the beginning of a word.

◄ prove
prove
provision
race
radar
radiation
radio
railroad
rain
raise
random
range
rank
rapid
rare
rate
rather
raw
reach
react
read
ready
realistic
rear
reason
receive
recent
recognize
recommendation
record
recreation
red
reduce
refer
refine
reform
refrigerator
refuge
refund

refuse
regard
regime
regiment
region
register
rehabilitation
relationship
relief
remain
remark
remember
remote
remove
render
rent
repair
repeat
report
represent
reputation
require
research
reserve
residence
resist
resource
respect
respond
response
rest
restaurant
restrict
resume
retain
retire
return
reveal
revenue

rhythm
rice
rich
rid
ride
right
rigid
ring
rise
risk
river
road
rock
roll
romantic
roof
room
root
rose
rough
round
route
routine
row
run
rush
Russia
screen
screw
spread
spring
straight
strain
strange
strategic
strategy
stream
street
stress   ►

INITIAL CONSONANT r* (CONTINUED)

◄

stretch	tradition	tremble
strict	traffic	tremendous
strike	tragedy	trend
string	trail	trial
strip	train	tribute
stroke	trait	trim
strong	transfer	trip
struck	transform	triumph
structure	transition	troop
threat	transportation	trouble
through	trap	truck
throughout	travel	trust
thrown	treasury	truth
trace	treat	try
track	treatment	written†
tractor	treaty	wrong†
trade	tree	wrote†

MEDIAL CONSONANT r

abroad	appropriate	authority
abstract	approve	average
accurate	approximate	bureau
across	arbitrary	carriage
address	area	carrier
administration	arise	carry
agree	around	category
America	arouse	century
angry	arrange	character
anniversary	arrest	comparison
apparatus	arrive	compromise
apparent	artery	concentrate
appreciate	astronomy	conference
approach	attractive	confront

►

*As the initial sound or in a consonant combination at the beginning of a word.
†When the *wr* spelling pattern occurs at the beginning of a syllable or word, the *w* is silent.

◄ congregate
congress
considerate
consideration
conspiracy
construction
contemporary
contract
contrary
contrast
contribute
controversy
corporation
correct
correspond
country
courage
curious
current
degree
democratic
demonstrate
depression
describe
description
desperate
destroy
destruction
dictionary
different
direct
direction
director
discovery
discriminate
distraction
distribution
district
doctrine

during
encourage
enterprise
entrance
entry
era
error
Europe
every
experience
experiment
expression
extra
extraordinary
extreme
fabric
factory
favorite
foreign
forest
generation
generous
hatred
hero
history
horizon
hundred
hungry
hurry
hydrogen
impress
improve
increase
incredible
industry
inherit
injury
instruction
instrument

insurance
integration
interest
interference
interior
interpretation
introduce
inventory
January
jury
literary
majority
marine
marriage
maturity
memory
merit
minority
mirror
misconstrue
mystery
narrative
narrow
necessary
numerous
obstruction
opera
operate
operation
orchestra
parade
parents
Paris
period
poetry
reference
sacrifice
satisfactory
secret ►

MEDIAL CONSONANT r (CONTINUED)

◄
secretary	summary	theory
security	superior	thorough
segregate	supreme	tomorrow
separate	surprise	variation
series	surrender	variety
serious	surround	various
sheriff	temperature	very
sorry	temporary	victory
sovereign	terrain	vigorous
spirit	terrible	warrant
story	territory	worry

CONSONANTS r AND l IN THE SAME WORD

agricultural	editorial	military
already	elaborate	milligram
apparently	electric	mineral
approval	empirical	moral
approximately	favorable	natural
April	federal	neutral
barrel	Florida	oral
brilliant	frequently	original
bronchial	general	patrol
Brooklyn	glory	planetary
central	gradually	practical
children	historical	preliminary
chlorine	illustrate	presently
clarity	imperial	primarily
comparable	increasingly	principle
control	industrial	probable
crawl	jewelry	problem
criminal	laboratory	professional
critical	liberal	promptly
crucial	library	proposal
crystal	literally	pulmonary
currently	literature	racial
deliberately	material	radical
delivery	metropolitan	rapidly

►

◄ rational
real
realize
really
recall
recently
reflect
reflection
regardless
regional
regular
related
relation
relative
release
relevant

reliable
relieved
religion
removal
replace
reply
republican
residential
resolution
respectively
responsibility
result
reveal
revolution
riffle
ritual

role
royal
rule
salary
slavery
strongly
struggle
temporarily
theoretical
traditional
travel
trial
trouble
voluntary

Phrases: *r*

AUDIO

4.3

Listen to the recording of the following phrases, then read the phrases aloud. Concentrate on correctly pronouncing the r sound, which is marked phonetically.

      r   r
1 addressing depression

        r   r
2 satisfactory parenting

     r   r
3 impressive poetry

       r   r
4 numerous memories

     r   r
5 every experience

     r   r
6 improved drastically

    r   r
7 heroic treatment

8 t<u>r</u>emendous t<u>r</u>adition

9 di<u>r</u>ecting g<u>r</u>eat ope<u>r</u>a

10 f<u>r</u>equent <u>r</u>elief

11 p<u>r</u>essure to <u>r</u>eturn

12 sp<u>r</u>eading st<u>r</u>ange <u>r</u>umors

13 st<u>r</u>eaming <u>r</u>ecordings

14 <u>r</u>efused to <u>r</u>ush

15 sepa<u>r</u>ate sto<u>r</u>ies

16 su<u>r</u>render the invento<u>r</u>y

17 int<u>r</u>oducing a dist<u>r</u>action

18 na<u>r</u>row majo<u>r</u>ity

19 co<u>r</u>responding inte<u>r</u>est

20 app<u>r</u>oved ope<u>r</u>ation

Sentences: *r*

Listen to the recording of the following sentences, then read the sentences aloud. Concentrate on correctly pronouncing the r sound, which is marked phonetically.

AUDIO
4.4

1 The p<u>r</u>og<u>r</u>am di<u>r</u>ector c<u>r</u>eated <u>r</u>evenue without <u>r</u>aising p<u>r</u>ices.

2 Will the c<u>r</u>owd pay t<u>r</u>ibute to the cou<u>r</u>ageous he<u>r</u>o?

3 C<u>r</u>ime level cont<u>r</u>ibutes d<u>r</u>amatically to a count<u>r</u>y's tou<u>r</u>ism indust<u>r</u>y.

4 Branches of the frozen tree broke off and struck the trailer.

5 I really hate driving through rush-hour traffic!

6 The children rarely rested during spring break.

7 Precision in preparation precedes growth and improvement.

8 Rita and Rick have a travel tradition: a road trip through the countryside.

9 The entrepreneur reserved a private room at a reputable restaurant.

10 Rice isn't rich in complete protein, but provides nutrients.

11 Tristan's professor remarked, "Resist propaganda, but promote reform!"

12 Research recommends recreation to rejuvenate and reduce stress.

13 A strategic response can transform trouble into triumph.

14 Andrew was not ready to retire, so he resisted the pressure.

15 The preventative treatment required a rather tricky procedure.

16 Provisions for breakfast included bread and dried fruit.

17 I presume the precious mineral rocks could be crafted into refined jewelry.

18 Can the agreement bring relief to the strained relationships?

19 Robert misconstrued his doctrine as correct, superior—and not rigid!

20 Rough terrain surrounded the trail that stretched along the marine.

Phrases: *r* vs. *l*

AUDIO
🎧
4.5

Listen to the recording of the following phrases, then read the phrases aloud. Concentrate on distinguishing between the r and l sounds, which are marked phonetically.

    r   l   r l
1 revealing the rules

   lr   r l
2 already relieved

  r   l r
3 raining in Florida

    r   r l l
4 attractive travel plan

    r   l l r
5 increasingly liberal

   r   r l   r l
6 primarily favorable

    l   r r l
7 voluntary release

  r   l r   l
8 royal ritual

  r l   r l
9 relevant reply

    r   l r l
10 traditional role

   l   r   r l l
11 elaborate but reliable

      r r l   r   l
12 temporarily struggling

    r   l r   l
13 original principle

    l r l r   l
14 deliberately practical

   r   l r
15 trouble trusting

   l r   r l
16 glorious reflection

  r   l r l
17 responsible relative

    l r   r l
18 mi<u>li</u>ta<u>ry</u> gene<u>ral</u>

    r l   r   l
19 <u>r</u>ea<u>l</u>izes <u>r</u>esponsibi<u>l</u>ity

    r   l   r l
20 <u>r</u>esu<u>l</u>ting <u>r</u>eso<u>l</u>ution

Sentences: *r* vs. *l*

AUDIO 4.6

Listen to the recording of the following sentences, then read the sentences aloud. Concentrate on distinguishing between the r and l sounds, which are marked phonetically.

      r   l   r l   r   r l   r
1 My <u>r</u>ambunctious fe<u>l</u>ine, <u>Ri</u>ley, th<u>r</u>ived on app<u>r</u>ova<u>l</u> and t<u>r</u>eats.

    r   l   r   r l l l   l   r   l
2 B<u>r</u>uce's c<u>l</u>ient <u>r</u>emained <u>r</u>e<u>l</u>ative<u>l</u>y f<u>l</u>exib<u>l</u>e and p<u>r</u>ofessiona<u>l</u>.

          r   l r   l   r   l   r
3 Is their p<u>r</u>oposa<u>l</u> p<u>r</u>actica<u>l</u>, conside<u>r</u>ing the substantia<u>l</u> moneta<u>r</u>y

     r
    sac<u>r</u>ifices?

    r l   l r r   l   r   l   r   l
4 <u>R</u>e<u>l</u>ax—a sa<u>l</u>a<u>r</u>y <u>r</u>aise <u>l</u>ooks inc<u>r</u>easing<u>l</u>y p<u>r</u>obab<u>l</u>e!

           l   r   l l   r   r   r l
5 The dip<u>l</u>omatic st<u>r</u>ugg<u>l</u>e i<u>ll</u>ust<u>r</u>ated the inhe<u>r</u>ent p<u>r</u>ob<u>l</u>ems of an

    l   r   l
    e<u>l</u>ementa<u>r</u>y so<u>l</u>ution.

    r   r l   l   l   l r   r   l   r l
6 <u>R</u>eed <u>r</u>e<u>l</u>uctantly faci<u>l</u>itated de<u>l</u>ive<u>r</u>y of the c<u>r</u>itica<u>l</u> mate<u>r</u>ia<u>l</u> for the

    r l r
    t<u>r</u>ia<u>l</u> p<u>r</u>ocedure.

       l   r   r   r   l l   l   r   l   l
7 The e<u>l</u>abo<u>r</u>ate <u>r</u>use was <u>r</u>idicu<u>l</u>ously convo<u>l</u>uted and <u>r</u>esu<u>l</u>ted in fai<u>l</u>ure.

        l   r l   l   l   l   r   l   r l
8 A <u>l</u>ess than b<u>r</u>i<u>ll</u>iant conc<u>l</u>usion exp<u>l</u>ains <u>L</u>on's and <u>R</u>on's <u>l</u>osing cont<u>r</u>ol

         r
    of the p<u>r</u>oject.

    r   r   r   l   r   r   r l
9 <u>R</u>ain in sp<u>r</u>ing p<u>r</u>oduced <u>l</u>uscious g<u>r</u>owth in the <u>r</u>oses on the t<u>r</u>e<u>ll</u>is.

     r l r   l   l   r l   r   l

10 Industrial-strength cleaning supplies are crucial for thoroughly

  l   r

cleaning the residence.

      l r   l   r l   r   l l   r

11 The clarity of the plan relieved me from my felt obligation to worry.

       r   r   l   l r   l

12 The opera's recitatives were simultaneously rhythmic and melodious.

   l   l   r   r   l l r l

13 "Silence is golden," Ruth remarked after a particularly grueling

        r   l

conference call.

  r l   r   r   l   r   r   l

14 Troubled, angry, and brooding male characters are frequently

r r   l

represented in films.

    l   r   r l l   r l   r   r

15 Can we please reach a crystal-clear preliminary agreement by the

     r l   l

federal holiday?

    r l r   r   r   l r   •r   r   l l

16 Empirical proof requires original research through practical planning.

    l r   r   l r l   r l   l   r l l

17 Children frequently rely on the natural impulse of role-playing.

    r l   r l   l   l   r   r

18 Harold's relatives loved his blue cheese dip and requested that he bring

  l

plenty.

    l   r l   r l   r   l r   l

19 Implementing the new resolution resulted in the gradual removal

  r   l r l

of radical rules.

   r l   l r   r l   r l   r

20 Generally, most people respond favorably to approval and recognition.

FIVE

The consonant *l*

The *l* sound defined

The consonant *l*, represented by the phonetic symbol l, frequently presents a challenge to nonnative speakers of English. Depending on your native language, you may pronounce l too "darkly," with the entire front of your tongue pressed up against the roof of your mouth; this is called velar l. Or your lips may try to pronounce l by rounding, when your tongue doesn't lift. Both placements are incorrect.

Step 1: Feeling the placement of *l*

Turn now to **Video Track 9,** where a step-by-step demonstration of the placement of l is presented. After you have watched the video, read the following description of the sound placement and do the exercises below.

VIDEO

9

Take out your mirror. Let's examine the position of the tongue in forming the consonant l. Looking in the mirror, place the tip of your tongue against your lower teeth, with your tongue lying flat on the floor of your mouth. To form the l correctly, lift your tongue, and place only the tip against the alveolar ridge, just behind your upper teeth. Make sure that your tongue is not touching the back of your upper teeth and that you are using only the tip of your tongue against the alveolar ridge. Now, say l.

Do not round your lips when saying l. Your lips should not move at all during the production of this sound. You can check yourself by placing your index finger against your lips, as demonstrated on the video.

49

Again looking in the mirror, watch the movement of your tongue. The tip begins against your lower teeth. Relax your lips, put only the tip of your tongue against the alveolar ridge, and say l.

Return now to **Video Track 9**. Practice the correct placement of the consonant l.

Step 2: Hearing the placement of *l*

Using the mirror, look closely inside your mouth. Begin by making a velar l, whose phonetic symbol is ł. Place the entire front of your tongue against the roof of your mouth. Exaggerate by using force as you push your tongue against the hard palate. As you feel the body of your tongue tense, listen for the dark, thick sound that results as you say ł.

Now, relax your tongue on the floor of your mouth, and using very little effort, lift the tip to the alveolar ridge, and say *la-la-la-la*. Notice how relaxed this position feels—and how much lighter this l sounds. Go back and forth between these two positions: your tongue tensed against the hard palate (ł), then your tongue lightly touching the alveolar ridge: ł . . . l . . . ł . . . l.

Watch in the mirror as you pronounce the pairs of words in the following list. Listen to the differences between l and ł, so that you can train your ear to hear the distinction, as well as feel the physiological difference in placement.

Note: In previous chapters, the correct sound placement for a consonant was contrasted with another frequently substituted phoneme of English. There are no words in English, however, that use a velar ł. Therefore, the words in the list below are the same in both columns. The purpose of the exercise is to pronounce each word incorrectly with a velar ł, then correctly with an alveolar l. The difference between the two is recorded on the accompanying recording.

ł	l
lead	lead (*present-tense verb*)
lie	lie
link	link
load	load ►

ł	l
led	led
lash	lash
low	low
loud	loud
lime	lime
blink	blink
class	class
clear	clear
clam	clam
live	live (*adjective*)
lip	lip

AUDIO
5.1

*Turn now to **Audio Track 5.1**, which features the sound adjustments between ł and l. Repeat the pairs of words, while comparing your pronunciation with that on the recording.*

Record your own pronunciation, and compare it to the audio track. Repeat this exercise until you feel ready to proceed to the next step.

Step 3: Applying the placement of *l*

Following are lists of common English words that contain the l consonant. You can practice this sound by checking your pronunciation against the word list recordings. After you have mastered the sound, advance to the phrases. Then move on to the sentences.

AUDIO
5.2

INITIAL l*

black	claim	clinical
blame	class	clock
blanket	classic	close
blind	clay	cloth
block	clean	clothes
blonde	clear	cloud
blood	clerk	club
blow	climate	flash
blue	climb	flat

*As the initial sound or in a consonant combination at the beginning of a word.

INITIAL l* (CONTINUED)

◄

flax	leader	loan
fled	league	lobby
flesh	lean	locate
flexible	leap	lock
flight	learn	logical
floor	least	London
flow	leather	lonely
flower	leave	long
flu	led	look
fluid	left	loop
flux	leg	loose
fly	legal	lose
glad	legend	loss
glance	legislation	lost
glass	length	loud
label	less	love
lack	lesson	low
ladder	let	loyalty
lady	letter	luck
laid	level	lumber
lake	liberty	lunch
land	lie	lungs
lane	lieutenant	luxury
language	life	placate
languid	lift	place
large	light	placid
last	like	plain
late	limit	plan
Latin	line	plane
latter	linear	planet
laugh	liquid	plant
law	list	plaster
lawyer	listen	plastic
lay	live	plate
lead	load	platform

►

*As the initial sound or in a consonant combination at the beginning of a word.

◄ play   plus   slip
  pleasant   slave   slow
  please   sleep   splendid
  pleasure   slender   splice
  plenty   slide   split
  plot   slight
  plug   slim

MEDIAL *l*

ability	below	declaration
absolute	billion	declare
accomplish	biology	decline
alert	bullet	delay
alienation	calculate	delicate
alike	calendar	delight
alive	California	deliver
alliance	capability	development
allies	ceiling	dilemma
allotment	cellar	diplomatic
allow	challenge	discipline
almost	cholesterol	displacement
alone	civilian	display
along	civilization	dollar
also	colleague	early
alter	collection	easily
alternative	college	elect
although	colony	election
altogether	color	element
always	column	eleven
analysis	complain	eliminate
applied	complement	else
Atlantic	complete	elsewhere
available	complicate	elusion
balance	conclude	employ
ballet	conclusion	employee
belief	conflict	English
believe	culture	enliven
belong	daily	envelope

►

MEDIAL l (CONTINUED)

◄ equivalent
establish
evaluation
excellent
exclusive
explain
explicit
exploration
facility
faculty
failure
familiar
family
fellow
follow
formula
gallery
gentleman
golden
guilty
helpless
holiday
holy
ideology
illness
illustration
implicate
inclined
include
influence
intellect
intelligent
involved
island
isolate
July
melody

milligram
million
morality
nevertheless
nuclear
obligation
only
ourselves
outlook
palace
parallel
particular
pathology
peculiar
personality
philosophy
pilot
police
policy
politics
politician
popular
population
possibility
probability
psychology
public
publicity
qualified
quality
salvation
scholar
select
settlement
shelter
shoulder
silence

silver
similar
simultaneous
socialist
soldier
solely
solemn
solid
solution
specialist
spectacular
supplement
supply
surplus
symbolic
talent
technology
telegraph
telephone
television
theology
ugly
ultimate
utility
valley
value
velocity
violence
violet
volume
volunteer
welcome
welfare
wildlife
yellow

FINAL *l**

able	channel	example
acceptable	chapel	external
accessible	chemical	fail
actual	child	false
additional	civil	feel
all	clinical	fell
amicable	coal	felt
angel	cold	female
angle	colonel	festival
animal	comfortable	field
annual	commercial	file
appeal	continental	fill
article	continual	film
assemble	control	final
automobile	conventional	financial
ball	cool	fiscal
battle	council	foil
beautiful	couple	fool
bell	cycle	formal
belt	deal	full
Bible	detail	functional
bill	devil	fundamental
binomial	difficult	funeral
bold	disposal	gentle
bottle	double	girl
bowl	doubtful	goal
build	dull	golf
call	economical	guilt
capable	emotional	gulf
capital	entitled	hall
capitol	equal	handle
careful	essential	health
casual	eternal	heel
cattle	eventual	held
cell	evil	hell

►

*As the final sound or in a consonant combination at the end of a word.

FINAL l* (CONTINUED)

◄ help	middle	potential
herself	mile	powerful
hill	milk	practical
hold	mill	pull
hole	missile	pupil
hospital	mobile	recall
hotel	model	resolve
hurdle	motel	riffle
ideal	multiple	saddle
impossible	municipal	sail
impulse	muscle	sale
individual	mutual	salt
install	myself	sample
internal	national	scale
international	navel	schedule
interval	noble	school
involve	normal	self
itself	notable	sell
jail	novel	settle
journal	occasional	several
kill	official	shall
little	oil	shell
local	old	signal
mail	pale	single
male	panel	skill
marble	partial	small
martial	particle	smell
marvel	pencil	smile
material	people	social
meal	personal	soil
medical	physical	sold
melt	pile	solve
memorial	pistol	soul
mental	pool	special
metal	possible	spiritual ►

*As the final sound or in a consonant combination at the end of a word.

◄ staple

staple
startle
steal
still
style
substantial
subtle
successful
suitable
survival
symbol
table
tale
tall
tangible
technical
tell

temple
textile
told
viable
thermal
tool
total
twelve
typical
uncle
universal
until
useful
usual
variable
vehicle
verbal

virtual
visible
visual
vital
wall
wealth
well
wheel
while
whole
wild
will
wonderful
world
yield

Phrases: *l*

Listen to the recording of the following phrases, then read the phrases aloud. Concentrate on correctly pronouncing the l sound, which is marked phonetically.

AUDIO
5.3

1 wealthy and successful people

2 totally typical

3 wonderful wildlife

4 especially crucial lesson

5 universal symbolism

6 several sample sales

7 notable clinical trial

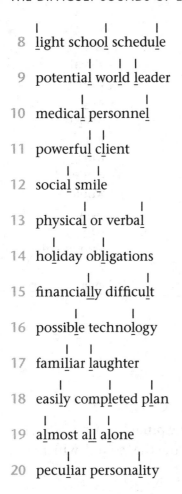

8 light school schedule

9 potential world leader

10 medical personnel

11 powerful client

12 social smile

13 physical or verbal

14 holiday obligations

15 financially difficult

16 possible technology

17 familiar laughter

18 easily completed plan

19 almost all alone

20 peculiar personality

Sentences: l

*Turn to **Audio Track 5.4**.* Listen to the recording of the following sentences, then read the sentences aloud. Concentrate on correctly pronouncing the l sound, which is marked phonetically.

AUDIO
5.4

1 I could tell at a glance that Larry learned less from the lesson than Lily.

2 A lack of blame allowed the couple to avoid battle and settle amicably.

3 Full accessibility to the hospital is essential if the clinical trial is

   to be successful.

4 The lighting was functional, but romantic and lovely.

5 Animals are like people—social when handled gently.

6 Linda was startled at the substantial cost of a suitable lawyer.

7 I love Louis Armstrong's recording of "What a Wonderful World."

8 Without a plan, it's a long leap from possible to probable success.

9 Will you fly to Los Angeles for a lengthy holiday?

10 Listen carefully, and eventually you will conclude that Lena is less

     than logical.

11 Is it practical for Bill to finalize the commercially viable real estate deal?

12 It's financially impossible to assemble additional automobiles

     at the plant.

13 Melinda has gotten slightly slimmer and her clothes look large on her.

14 I longed for the pleasantly cool fall climate by the lake in Lucerne.

15 The employee was labeled as placid, but I believe he's lazy.

16 What languages will develop in civilizations and cultures of the future?

17 Play in life, and health and laughter will follow.

18 The lieutenant's letter listed losses that could easily lead to a costly

     lawsuit.

19 Challenging hurdles and difficult dilemmas always enliven Louie.

20 My colleague's complaints complicated the completion of this

particular evaluation.

SIX

The consonant *ng* (ŋ)

Fred was practicing his English pronunciation more often and was beginning to enjoy the sound of his voice. He worked on his *l* placement by vocalizing on *la-la-la-la.* When he saw his colleague Margaret on the elevator, Fred told her of his practice. "Margaret," he confessed, "I'm sinning all the time!"

The *ŋ* sound defined

The consonant *ng*, represented by the phonetic symbol ŋ, is almost always mispronounced by nonnative speakers of English. This is because the spelling pattern is deceptive: Most individuals pronounce the *n*, followed by a separate *g*. So it was with Fred, who meant to say *singing* instead of *sinning*. But this *ng* spelling pattern in English represents a single phoneme, and its sound is formed in a very different place than that of the consonant *n*. Additionally, this sound is used in the spelling pattern *nk*. When used in an *ng* spelling pattern, only ŋ is sounded. There are some exceptions to this rule, notably when the *ng* spelling is in the root of the word (as in *angle*) and when it occurs in the comparative and superlative forms of an adjective (as in *stronger* and *strongest*). In these instances, the g is sounded in addition to the ŋ phoneme. These exceptions are marked in the following word lists. In an *nk* spelling pattern, the k is always sounded as a separate phoneme: ŋk.

Step 1: Feeling the placement of *ŋ*

VIDEO 10

Turn now to **Video Track 10,** where a step-by-step demonstration of the placement of ŋ is presented. After you have watched the video, read the following description of the sound placement and do the exercises below.

Take out your mirror. Let's examine the position of the tongue in forming the consonant ŋ. Looking in the mirror, place the tip of your tongue against your lower teeth, with your tongue lying flat on the floor of your mouth. First, we will make an n sound, as a contrast to ŋ. Lift the tip of your tongue, place it against the alveolar ridge, and say n . . . *win.*

Now, let's try ŋ. Place the tip of your tongue against your lower teeth, then raise the back of your tongue until it touches the soft palate, as you do for the consonants k and g. Say k . . . g. Now, lower your tongue to the floor of your mouth again, with the tip of your tongue against your lower teeth. Touch the back of your tongue to the soft palate again, and holding it there, allow the sound to be released through your nose. Say ŋ.

Avoid the tendency to pull your entire tongue backward. You can check yourself by holding the front and middle of your tongue down using the tip of your little finger, as demonstrated on the video. Raise only the back of your tongue, and say ŋ . . . *wing.*

Return now to **Video Track 10.** Practice the correct placement of the consonant ŋ.

Step 2: Hearing the placement of *ŋ*

Using your mirror, look closely inside your mouth. Place the tip of your tongue against the alveolar ridge, and say n. You will hear this sound as both nasal and very forward in the mouth. Now, anchor your tongue against your lower teeth, raise only the back of your tongue until it touches the soft palate, and say ŋ. You will hear a nasal sound here too, but it is realized at the back of the throat. Go back and forth between the two placements: n . . . ŋ . . . n . . . ŋ.

Watch in the mirror as you pronounce the pairs of words in the following lists. Listen to the differences in the consonant sounds, so that you can train your ear to hear the distinction, as well as feel the physiological difference in placement.

n	ŋ
ba<u>n</u>	ba<u>ng</u>
di<u>n</u>	di<u>ng</u>
fa<u>n</u>	fa<u>ng</u>
si<u>n</u>	si<u>ng</u>
ra<u>n</u>	ra<u>ng</u>
pa<u>n</u>	pa<u>ng</u>
ki<u>n</u>	ki<u>ng</u>
stu<u>n</u>	stu<u>ng</u>
thi<u>n</u>	thi<u>ng</u>
su<u>n</u>	su<u>ng</u>

n	ŋk
ba<u>n</u>	ba<u>nk</u>
cla<u>n</u>	cla<u>nk</u>
fu<u>n</u>	fu<u>nk</u>
i<u>n</u>	i<u>nk</u>
ra<u>n</u>	ra<u>nk</u>
si<u>n</u>	si<u>nk</u>
su<u>n</u>	su<u>nk</u>
ta<u>n</u>	ta<u>nk</u>
thi<u>n</u>	thi<u>nk</u>
wi<u>n</u>	wi<u>nk</u>

AUDIO
6.1

*Turn now to **Audio Track 6.1**,* which features the sound adjustments between n and ŋ. Repeat the pairs of words, while comparing your pronunciation with that on the recording.

Record your own pronunciation, and compare it to the audio track. Repeat this exercise until you feel ready to proceed to the next step.

Step 3: Applying the placement of ŋ

Following are lists of common English words that contain the ŋ consonant. You can practice this sound by checking your pronunciation against the word list recordings. After you have mastered the sound, advance to the phrases. Then move on to the sentences.

Note that the ŋ sound does not occur at the beginning of a word in English.

AUDIO
6.2

MEDIAL ŋ

anchor	finger*	shingle*
anger*	function	singer
angle*	fungus*	single*
anguish*	gangster	singular*
ankle	hanging	spangle*
anxiety	hunger*	springing
banging	junction	sprinkle
bangle*	language*	stinger
bankrupt	languid*	strangle*
banquet	languish*	stringing
bingo*	linger*	stronger*
blanket	lingo*	strongest*
bronchial	linguist*	swinging
bungalow*	longer*	tangle*
canker	longest*	tango*
cantankerous	manganese*	tincture
conquer	mangle*	tingle*
cranky	mango*	tinkle
crinkle	mingle*	triangle*
dangle*	monkey	trinket
disjunction	punctual	twinkle
distinguish*	punctuation	uncle
donkey	puncture	unction
dungaree*	rancor	vanquish
elongate*	rectangle*	wrangle*
embankment	sanctimonious	Yankee
extinguish*	sanction	

*In these words, the *g* is pronounced after the ŋ phoneme.

FINAL ŋ*

-ing (*suffix*)	flank	punk
along	fling	rang
among	flung	rank
anything	flunk	ring
bang	frank	rink
bank	funk	rung
belong	gang	sacrosanct
blank	hang	sang
blink	harangue	sank
boomerang	honk	shrank
bring	hung	shrink
brink	hunk	sing
Bronx	ink	sink
bunk	inning	skunk
chink	instinct	slang
clang	king	sling
clank	kink	slink
cling	larynx	slung
clink	length	song
clothing	lightning	spank
clung	link	sphinx
dank	living	sprang
debunk	long	spring
defunct	lung	sprung
ding	meringue	spunk
diphthong	mink	sting
distinct	monk	stink
drink	nothing	stocking
dunk	oblong	strength
during	pang	string
dwelling	pharynx	strong
evening	plank	strung
everything	plunk	stung
extinct	prolong	succinct
fang	prong	sung

►

*As the final sound or in a consonant combination at the end of a word.

FINAL ŋ (CONTINUED)

◄	sunk	throng	wing
	swank	tong	wink
	swing	tongue	wrong
	tank	triphthong	yank
	thank	trunk	young
	thing	twang	zinc
	think	wedding

Phrases: ŋ

AUDIO

6.3

Listen to the recording of the following phrases, then read the phrases aloud. Concentrate on correctly pronouncing the ŋ sound, which is marked phonetically.

      ŋg   ŋg
1 the English language

     ŋ   ŋ
2 nothing doing

   ŋ ŋ   ŋ
3 singing strongly

    ŋ ŋ   ŋk
4 clanging and clanking

    ŋk   ŋk
5 uncle's blanket

    ŋk   ŋ
6 stinky stocking

    ŋg   ŋk
7 stronger drink

    ŋg   ŋ
8 mango pudding

    ŋk   ŋ
9 thinking of procrastinating

   ŋ ŋ   ŋ
10 bringing nothing

11 belo[ŋ]ed to a ga[ŋ]g

12 a lo[ŋ]ng, lo[ŋ]ng so[ŋ]ng

13 a to[ŋ]ngue lashi[ŋ]ng

14 a cra[ŋk]nky mo[ŋk]nkey

15 recta[ŋg]ngular pla[ŋk]nk

16 belo[ŋ]ngi[ŋ]ng in the tru[ŋk]nk

17 pu[ŋk]nctual si[ŋ]nger

18 tria[ŋg]ngular tri[ŋk]nket

19 ti[ŋg]ngling fi[ŋg]nger

20 disti[ŋg]nguished Ya[ŋk]nkee

Sentences: ŋ

*Turn to **Audio Track 6.4**. Listen to the recording of the following sentences, then read the sentences aloud. Concentrate on correctly pronouncing the ŋ sound, which is marked phonetically.

AUDIO
6.4

1 A ta[ŋg]ngle of weeds grew alo[ŋ]ng the emba[ŋk]nkment.

2 Where is the tip of your to[ŋ]ngue for all diphtho[ŋ]ngs?

3 We sa[ŋ]ng alo[ŋ]ng with a lo[ŋ]ng so[ŋ]ng at the skati[ŋ]ng ri[ŋk]nk.

4 The you[ŋ]ng company was on the bri[ŋk]nk of ba[ŋk]nkruptcy.

5 I'm looki[ŋ]ng forward to dini[ŋ]ng at the ba[ŋk]nquet.

     ŋk   ŋk   ŋ   ŋk
6 Frank functioned well when relying on instinct.

     ŋg   ŋ   ŋg
7 Linger by the fire—the kindling's flame isn't extinguished.

         ŋ   ŋk   ŋk   ŋ
8 We should bring hot drinks and blankets on the outing.

           ŋ   ŋ ŋ   ŋk ŋ
9 What is that annoying clanging and clanking sound?

      ŋg   ŋk
10 She was angry when her car tire was punctured.

   ŋk ŋ   ŋ
11 Flunking a crucial test can produce anxiety.

    ŋ   ŋk   ŋg   ŋk ŋ
12 Bring the anchor at a closer angle before sinking it.

    ŋg   ŋ   ŋ
13 We mingled with the singers all evening.

    ŋk   ŋ   ŋks
14 My uncle owns a housing unit in the Bronx.

   ŋk   ŋ ŋ   ŋ   ŋ
15 Slinky and clinging clothing can be flattering.

       ŋ   ŋ
16 In the spring, turn your clocks forward for daylight savings time.

     ŋk   ŋ   ŋk   ŋ
17 The stars twinkled along the embankment in the evening.

      ŋ   ŋ   ŋ ŋ
18 There's something soothing about living along the coast.

    ŋ   ŋg   ŋg   ŋ
19 Practicing the English language can prove rewarding.

   ŋk   ŋ   ŋ
20 Conquering fears prolongs careers.

Phrases: *ŋ* vs. *n*

AUDIO
6.5

    Listen to the recording of the following phrases, then read the phrases aloud. Concentrate on distinguishing between the ŋ and n sounds, which are marked phonetically.

     ŋ n   n
1 string instruments

    ŋ   n
2 you<u>ng</u> compa<u>n</u>y

    ŋg   n
3 hu<u>ng</u>ry for bru<u>n</u>ch

    ŋg   ŋ   n
4 exti<u>ng</u>uishi<u>ng</u> the ca<u>n</u>dle

    n ŋ   n ŋ
5 a wi<u>nn</u>i<u>ng</u> i<u>nn</u>i<u>ng</u>

    ŋg   ŋ   n
6 a<u>ng</u>ry you<u>ng</u> ma<u>n</u>

    n ŋk   n
7 i<u>n</u>sti<u>nc</u>tive i<u>n</u>dividual

    n   ŋg
8 i<u>n</u>dex fi<u>ng</u>er

    ŋk   n   ŋ
9 tha<u>nk</u>ful for <u>n</u>early everythi<u>ng</u>

     n   ŋ
10 <u>n</u>ot a diphtho<u>ng</u>

     ŋk   n   n
11 twi<u>nk</u>le i<u>n</u> the heave<u>n</u>s

     n   ŋ   n
12 <u>n</u>ice housi<u>ng</u> u<u>n</u>it

     n ŋ   n
13 wi<u>nn</u>i<u>ng</u> home ru<u>n</u>

     ŋ   n   n
14 a lu<u>ng</u> i<u>n</u>fectio<u>n</u>

     ŋ ŋ n   n
15 bri<u>ng</u>i<u>ng</u> <u>n</u>umerous <u>n</u>ecklaces

     n   ŋ n   n
16 <u>n</u>appi<u>ng</u> i<u>n</u> the <u>n</u>ursery

     n   n   ŋ
17 <u>n</u>utritio<u>n</u>al spri<u>ng</u> rolls

     ŋ   n
18 spru<u>ng</u> a <u>n</u>ew leak

     n   ŋk
19 <u>n</u>uclear exti<u>nc</u>tion

      ŋ   n n
20 prolo<u>ng</u>ed <u>n</u>ua<u>n</u>ce

Sentences: ŋ vs. n

Listen to the recording of the following sentences, then read the sentences aloud. Concentrate on distinguishing between the ŋ and n sounds, which are marked phonetically.

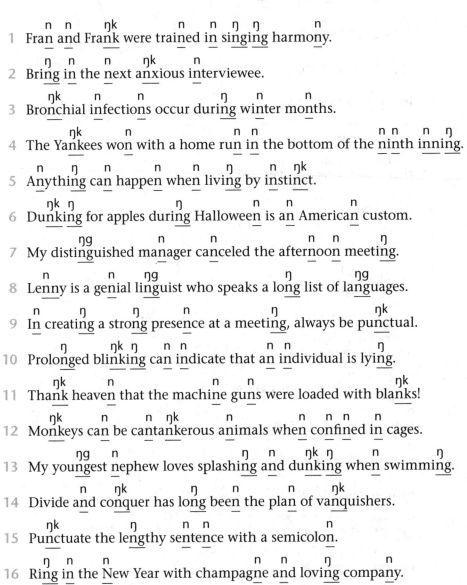

     n n   ŋk   n   n ŋ ŋ   n

1 Fran and Frank were trained in singing harmony.

    ŋ   n   n   ŋk   n

2 Bring in the next anxious interviewee.

    ŋk   n   n   ŋ   n   n

3 Bronchial infections occur during winter months.

       ŋk   n   n n   n n   n ŋ

4 The Yankees won with a home run in the bottom of the ninth inning.

    n   ŋ   n   n   n   ŋ   n ŋk

5 Anything can happen when living by instinct.

    ŋk ŋ   ŋ   n   n   n

6 Dunking for apples during Halloween is an American custom.

       ŋg   n   n   n n   ŋ

7 My distinguished manager canceled the afternoon meeting.

    n   n   ŋg   ŋ   ŋg

8 Lenny is a genial linguist who speaks a long list of languages.

    n   ŋ   ŋ   n   ŋ   ŋk

9 In creating a strong presence at a meeting, always be punctual.

      ŋ   ŋk ŋ   n n   n n   ŋ

10 Prolonged blinking can indicate that an individual is lying.

    ŋk   n   n   n   ŋk

11 Thank heaven that the machine guns were loaded with blanks!

    ŋk   n   n ŋk   n   n   n n   n

12 Monkeys can be cantankerous animals when confined in cages.

      ŋg   n   ŋ   n   ŋk ŋ   n   ŋ

13 My youngest nephew loves splashing and dunking when swimming.

      n ŋk   ŋ   n   n   ŋk

14 Divide and conquer has long been the plan of vanquishers.

    ŋk   ŋ   n n   n

15 Punctuate the lengthy sentence with a semicolon.

    ŋ   n   n   n   n   ŋ   n

16 Ring in the New Year with champagne and loving company.

17   Ken was wrong to sting Nancy with sanctimonious comments.

18   Don't cling to the proverbial anchor when trying not to sink.

19   My index finger was nearly mangled during the accident.

20   I long for the distinct ring of a robin's song in spring.

SEVEN

The consonants *b*, *v*, and *w*

The *b*, *v*, and *w* sounds defined

The consonants *b*, *v*, and *w*, represented by the phonetic symbols b, v, and w, are frequently mispronounced by nonnative speakers of English. Depending on the spelling patterns of your native language, you may mispronounce v as either b or w. Another common mistake is to mispronounce w as v.

While this may seem confusing at first, English is actually fairly consistent with spelling patterns for the phonemes b and v, which are represented by the English alphabet letters *b* and *v*.

The w sound may be a little trickier, as it not only represents a *w* spelling in English, but is usually found in the *qu* spelling pattern (phonetically, kw). Sometimes, the *u* spelling in the pattern *gu* is pronounced as w. Additionally, as indicated in Chapter Two (page 14), the w phoneme is always followed by a vowel. Therefore, the spelling of *w* is never a fully lip-rounded consonant phoneme w when it is used at the end of a syllable; instead, the spelling is often accounted for by the use of a vowel or diphthong, as in the words *law*, *snow*, and *down* (see Chapters Fifteen and Sixteen).

Step 1: Feeling the placement of *b, v,* and *w*

VIDEO
11

Turn now to **Video Track 11,** where a step-by-step demonstration of the placement of the consonants b, v, and w is presented. After you have watched the video, read the following description of the sound placements and do the exercises below.

Take out your mirror. Let's examine the position of the lips and upper teeth in forming the consonants b, v, and w. Looking in the mirror, place the tip of your tongue against your lower teeth, with your tongue resting on the floor of your mouth.

First, let's form a b. Put your lips together, apply a little pressure, pop them forward, and say b . . . *bill.* Now, return your lips to a neutral position. Place your lower lip against the bottom of your upper teeth, keep your upper lip completely still, and say v . . . *village.*

Last, put your upper and lower lips together, round them, and say w . . . *way.* Your upper teeth are not used in forming w.

Return now to **Video Track 11.** Practice the placement of the consonants b, v, and w.

Step 2: Hearing the placement of *b, v,* and *w*

Using your mirror, look closely at your lips and upper teeth. Place the tip of your tongue against your lower teeth. Say b . . . v . . . w, watching your lips and upper teeth for careful placement.

Watch in the mirror as you pronounce the pairs of words in the following lists. Listen to the differences in sounds, so that you can train your ear to hear the distinction, as well as feel the physiological difference in placement.

b	v
ban	van
brain	vain
banish	vanish
bat	vat
bent	vent
broke	evoke

►

b	v
◄ li<u>b</u>erty	li<u>v</u>ery
fi<u>b</u>er	fe<u>v</u>er
du<u>b</u>	do<u>v</u>e
stro<u>b</u>e	stro<u>v</u>e

AUDIO

7.1

*Turn now to **Audio Track 7.1**,* which features the sound adjustments between b and v. Repeat the pairs of words, while comparing your pronunciation with that on the recording.

Record your own pronunciation, and compare it to the audio track.

v	w
<u>v</u>ine	<u>w</u>ine
<u>V</u>in	<u>w</u>in
<u>v</u>est	<u>w</u>est
<u>v</u>eil	<u>w</u>ail
<u>v</u>ault	<u>w</u>all
<u>v</u>egetable	<u>w</u>edge
<u>v</u>erse	<u>w</u>orst
e<u>v</u>il	eq<u>u</u>al
fer<u>v</u>ent	freq<u>u</u>ent
pre<u>v</u>ent	pers<u>u</u>ade
in<u>v</u>ert	in<u>w</u>ard

AUDIO

7.2

*Turn now to **Audio Track 7.2**,* which features the sound adjustments between v and w. Repeat the pairs of words, while comparing your pronunciation with that on the recording.

Record your own pronunciation, and compare it to the audio track. Repeat this exercise until you feel ready to proceed to the next step.

Step 3: Applying the placement of *b, v,* and *w*

Following are lists of common English words that contain the b, v, and w consonants. You can practice these sounds by checking your pronunciation against the word list recordings. After you have mastered the sounds, advance to the phrases. Then move on to the sentences.

AUDIO
7.3

INITIAL b

babble	bead	biology
baboon	beam	bird
baby	bean	birth
bachelor	bear	bit
back	beast	bite
bacon	beat	bitter
bacteria	beautiful	bizarre
bad	because	black
badge	become	blade
baffle	bed	blame
bag	before	bland
baggage	beg	blank
bait	begin	blanket
bake	below	blast
balance	bend	blaze
balcony	benefactor	bleach
ball	benefit	bleak
ballad	berry	bleed
balloon	beside	bless
ballot	bet	blind
ban	betray	blink
band	better	bliss
bang	between	bloat
bank	beware	blob
banner	bewildered	block
bar	beyond	blood
bark	bias	blossom
barn	bib	blotch
barter	bibliography	blow
base	bicker	blubber
basis	bicycle	blue
basket	big	bluff
batch	bill	blunder
bate	billion	blunt
battery	billow	blur
battle	bin	board
beach	bind	boast

►

◄ boat | brag | brother
body | braid | brought
bogus | brain | brown
boil | brake | bruise
bold | brand | brunch
bolt | brass | brush
bomb | bread | brutal
bone | breadth | bubble
book | break | bucket
boom | breath | bud
boot | breathe | budget
booth | breed | bug
born | breeze | bulb
borrow | bribe | bulge
boss | brick | bulk
botch | bride | bull
both | bridge | bump
bottle | brief | bundle
bought | bright | burden
bounce | brilliant | bus
bound | bring | bush
bow | brochure | busy
bowl | broil | but
box | broke | button
boy | brood | buy
bracelet | brook | buzz
bracket | broom | by

MEDIAL b

-able (*suffix*) | abbey | abject
-ability (*suffix*) | abdicate | able
-ibility (*suffix*) | abdomen | abnormal
-ible (*suffix*) | abduct | aboard
aback | abhor | abolish
abandon | abide | abominable
abate | ability | about   ►

MEDIAL **b** (*CONTINUED*)

◄

abrasion	attribute	dubious
abroad	audible	durable
abrupt	cabinet	edible
absence	cable	elbow
absolute	caliber	eligible
abstain	capable	embargo
abstract	carbon	embark
absurd	chamber	embarrass
abundance	charitable	embellish
abuse	cobra	emblem
abyss	collaborate	embrace
acceptable	commendable	enable
accessible	comparable	ensemble
accountable	compatible	exacerbate
acrobat	comprehensible	excitable
adaptable	considerable	fabric
admirable	consumable	fabulous
admissible	corruptible	fallible
adorable	credible	feasible
aerobic	crumble	February
affable	cubicle	feeble
albeit	culpable	fiber
album	dabble	flexible
algebra	debate	forbid
ambassador	debilitate	gamble
amber	debit	habit
ambient	debris	hamburger
ambiguous	December	hobby
ambulance	delectable	hospitable
ambush	deliberate	humble
amicable	dependable	illegible
anybody	diabetes	imaginable
applicable	disability	impeccable
approachable	disposable	impossible
arbitrary	disputable	incredible
arbitration	distribute	incumbent
arbor	double	inhabit

►

◄ inhibit
intelligible
irritable
jumble
justifiable
label
labor
labyrinth
liable
liberal
library
limber
lobby
manageable
measurable
memorable
metabolism
miserable
mobile
negligible
negotiable
neighbor
nimble
noble
nobody
notable
number
obese
obey
obfuscate
obligate
oblige
obscene
obsolete
obstruct
obtain
obtrusion
October

ostensible
pebble
penetrable
perishable
phobia
placebo
plausible
pleasurable
pliable
possible
preferable
problem
public
publicity
publish
rabbit
rabble
rabid
ramble
rebate
rebel
regrettable
reimburse
reliable
reprehensible
republic
reputable
respectable
responsible
ribbon
robin
robot
robust
rubric
ruby
rumble
sabotage
satiable

scramble
scribble
sensible
September
shamble
sibling
slumber
somber
stable
stumble
subject
subjective
sublet
subsequent
subside
subsidiary
substance
substitute
subtract
suggestible
suitable
susceptible
syllable
syllabus
symbol
table
tabloid
taboo
tangible
taxable
tolerable
tremble
tribute
trouble
tumble
umbrage
umbrella
zebra

FINAL b*

absorb	job	slob
cab	knob	snob
club	mob	stab
crab	nab	stub
crib	prescribe	sub
cub	probe	tab
curb	rib	transcribe
ebb	rob	tribe
glib	robe	tub
globe	rub	tube
grab	scribe	
jab	scrub	

b AND v IN THE SAME WORD

abbreviate	convertible	variable
above	invincible	vegetable
absolve	irrevocable	venerable
abusive	November	verb
adverb	objective	verbatim
advisable	oblivion	verbiage
ambivalent	observe	verbose
available	obvious	viable
behavior	proverb	vibrant
believe	reverberate	vibrate
beloved	subjective	vocabulary
beverage	subservient	vulnerable
brave	subvert	
brevity	valuable	

INITIAL v†

svelte	vacation	vacillate
vacant	vaccinate	vacuum ►

---

*When the *mb* spelling pattern occurs at the end of a syllable or word, the *b* is silent; examples are *bomb*, *dumber*, and *lambskin*.

†As the initial sound or in a consonant combination at the beginning of a word.

◄ vagrant
vague
vain
valet
valiant
valid
valley
valor
valve
vampire
van
vandalize
vane
vanilla
vanish
vanity
vantage
vapid
vapor
variation
variety
various
varnish
varsity
vary
vascular
vase
vast
vat
vault
vegetarian
vehement
vehicle
veil
vein
velar
velocity
velvet

vendor
veneer
vengeance
venom
venerate
vent
ventilate
ventricle
venture
venue
verdict
verge
verify
vernacular
verse
version
versatile
versus
vertebra
vertical
vertigo
vest
veterinarian
veto
vex
vice
vicinity
vicious
victim
victory
vie
view
vigor
vile
vilify
village
villain
vindicate

vine
vinaigrette
vintage
violate
violent
violet
violin
virus
virtue
visa
visible
vision
visit
visualize
vital
vitamin
vivacious
vivid
vodka
vogue
voice
void
volatile
volcano
vulgar
volley
voltage
vulture
volume
volunteer
vortex
vote
vouch
vow
vowel
voyage

MEDIAL V

-ivity (*suffix*)	convalesce	divulge
activate	convene	drivel
advance	convenient	effervescent
advantage	conventional	elevate
adventure	conversation	eleven
adversary	conversion	endeavor
adverse	convert	envelope
advertise	convey	environment
advise	convict	envision
advocacy	convolute	envy
advocate	convulsion	evacuate
affidavit	cover	evade
aggravate	covet	evaluate
alleviate	crevice	evaporate
alveolar	cultivate	even
anniversary	deliver	evening
anvil	deprivation	event
avalanche	devalue	ever
avarice	devastate	evict
avenge	develop	evidence
avenue	deviate	evil
average	device	eviscerate
aversion	devil	evoke
avert	devious	evolve
aviation	devise	festival
avid	devoid	fever
avoid	devote	flavor
canvas	devour	frivolous
cavalier	disadvantage	galvanize
cavern	discover	government
caviar	diverge	gravity
cavity	diverse	gravy
cavort	divert	harvest
civic	divest	heaven
civilization	divide	heavy
clever	divine	improvise
conservation	divisible	individual
controversy	divorce	innovate ►

◄ interval

intervene

interview

invade

invent

invert

invest

invigorate

invite

invoice

invoke

ivory

ivy

juvenile

lavender

lavish

level

levity

liver

livid

malevolent

maneuver

maverick

medieval

navigate

navy

never

novel

novice

oval

oven

over

pavement

persevere

pervade

perverse

pivot

poverty

prevail

prevalent

prevent

preview

previous

privacy

privilege

privy

proclivity

provide

provoke

pulverize

ravenous

rejuvenate

renovation

reveal

revenge

revenue

reverence

review

revival

revoke

revulsion

rival

river

saliva

salvage

savage

saver

savvy

scavenge

servant

service

seven

sever

several

severance

severe

shovel

silver

souvenir

sovereign

supervise

television

travel

travesty

trivia

universe

FINAL V

-ative (*suffix*)

-ive (*suffix*)

achieve

active

adaptive

adjective

affirmative

alive

alternative

approve

archive

argumentative

arrive

assertive

attractive

calve

captive

carve

cave

clove

comparative

competitive

concave

conceive ►

FINAL **V** (CONTINUED)

◄ connive   give   passive
consecutive   glove   pejorative
contemplative   grave   positive
contrive   grieve   preserve
crave   groove   primitive
creative   grove   productive
cumulative   have   receive
deceive   heave   relative
decisive   hive   relieve
declarative   I've   remove
definitive   imperative   repetitive
delve   improve   reprieve
deprive   incisive   resolve
derisive   indicative   retrieve
derive   infinitive   revolve
deserve   initiative   sedative
disapprove   interrogative selective
dissolve   intuitive   sensitive
dive   leave   shave
dove   live   shelve
drive   love   shove
effective   lucrative   sieve
elective   motive   sleeve
elusive   move   solve
evolve   naïve   starve
executive   native   stove
figurative   negative   strive
five   nerve   survive
forgive   of*   tentative
fricative   offensive   thrive
fugitive   olive   you've

_____

*The _f_ of the English word _of_ is pronounced v.

V AND W IN THE SAME WORD

driveway	twelve	we've
suave	waive	weave
swerve	wave	whatever
swivel	waver	whenever

INITIAL W*

dwarf	swollen	wallet
dwell	swore	wallow
dwindle	thwart	walnut
one	tweak	walrus
suede	tweezers	waltz
suite	twenty	wander
swab	twice	want
swagger	twig	war
swallow	twilight	ward
swamp	twin	wardrobe
swan	twinge	warm
swank	twinkle	warning
swap	twirl	warp
swarthy	twist	warrant
swat	twitch	warrior
sway	twitter	wary
swear	wade	was
sweat	wafer	wash
sweep	waffle	Washington
sweet	wafture	wasn't
swell	wag	wasp
swelter	wage	waste
swift	wagon	watch
swim	waist	water
swindle	wait	watt
swirl	wake	wax
swish	walk	way
switch	wall	we ►

*As the initial sound or in a consonant combination at the beginning of a word.

INITIAL **W*** *(CONTINUED)*

◄

weak	when	wine
wealth	whether	wing
weapon	which	wink
wear	while	winter
weary	whimper	wipe
weather	whimsical	wire
web	whine	wisdom
wedding	whip	wish
wedge	whiskers	wisp
Wednesday	whisky	wit
weed	whisper	with
week	whistle	wither
weep	white	witness
weight	whiz	wobble
weird	why	woe
welcome	wick	woke
welfare	wide	wolf
well	widow	women
welt	width	won
went	wield	won't
wept	wife	wonder
were	wig	wool
west	wild	work
wet	will	worn
whale	willow	would
wharf	win	wouldn't
what	wince	wound
wheat	wind	wow
wheel	window	

MEDIAL **W**

afterward	anyone	await
always	anyway	awake
anguish	anywhere	award

►

*As the initial sound or in a consonant combination at the beginning of a word.

◄ aware
away
awhile
awkward
between
beware
bewildered
clockwise
clockwork
cobweb
crossword
distinguish
elsewhere

entwine
highway
Hollywood
inward
kilowatt
language
languid
languish
linguist
network
nowhere
onward
outward

outworn
penguin
reward
schwa
sidewalk
sideways
somewhat
somewhere
stalwart
subway
upward

W WITH *qu* SPELLING

acquaint
acquiesce
acquire
acquisition
acquit
adequate
antiquate
aquarium
bequeath
colloquial
equal
equate
equator
equipment
equity
equivalent
exquisite
frequent
inquire
inquisitive
kumquat
liquid
liquidate

loquacious
obsequious
quack
quad
quadrant
quadruple
quail
quaint
quake
qualify
quality
qualm
quantity
quarantine
quarrel
quarry
quart
quarter
quartet
quartz
quasi
queasy
queen

quench
query
quest
question
quibble
quick
quiet
quill
quilt
quinine
quintessence
quintuple
quip
quirk
quit
quite
quiver
quixotic
quiz
quota
quotation
request
requiem ►

W WITH *qu* SPELLING (*CONTINUED*)

◀ require	squalor	squeeze
requisite	squander	squelch
sequel	square	squid
sequence	squash	squint
sequester	squat	squirm
sequin	squawk	squirrel
squabble	squeak	squirt
squad	squeal	tranquil
squalid	squeamish	ubiquitous

Phrases: *b* vs. *v*

Listen to the recording of the following phrases, then read the phrases aloud. Concentrate on distinguishing between the b and v sounds, which are marked phonetically.

AUDIO
7.4

```
   b        v
1  balsamic vinaigrette

   b        v      b
2  abundant vocabulary

   v     b     b
3  valuable arbitration

        v   b        b
4  heavy boxes of books

   b v        b
5  above the lobby

   v      b     v
6  violent behavior

   v          b     b
7  vegetarian black beans

   v     b          b
8  vines blowing in the breeze

   v          b
9  visualized breathing

   v  v    b
10 velvet bracelet
```

        b v v
11 brave volunteer

        b   v v
12 subjective version

        b   v
13 a booming voice

        b   v
14 stubborn vampire

      v   b   b   b
15 valuable library book

        b   v
16 debating a victory

      v   b
17 vandalized cabinet

        b v   b
18 audible violin subsided

        b   v
19 October vacation

      b   b   v
20 bold blank verse

Sentences: *b* vs. *v*

AUDIO
7.5

    Listen to the recording of the following sentences, then read the sentences aloud. Concentrate on distinguishing between the b and v sounds, which are marked phonetically.

      b   v   b   v v   v
1 The billionaire served an abundance of caviar at his anniversary party.

   b v   v   b   b b   v   b
2 Beverly is available for babysitting in November.

                  b   b   v   v b
3 It's commendable when those with abundance volunteer to give back.

         v   v v b   b   v   v
4 Take advantage of vibrant, breathtaking views when vacationing.

      v   b v b   b v   b
5 The violin music audibly vibrated above the oboe.

   v   v   v   v   b   v   b
6 Vincent actively advocated having a more collaborative cabinet.

                    b   v b   b   v   v   b
  7 Are you capable of absorbing constructive and creative feedback?
              v   v   v b   b
  8 The movers heaved the heavy boxes into the brownstone.
          b   v   v   v   b b v
  9 I believe you'll love the new vegetable beverage.
              v b   b   v   b   b b
 10 It's advisable to abbreviate the bloated bibliography.
                  b   b   v   v
 11 Do you habitually breathe effectively? It's invigorating!
          b b   b   v   v   b
 12 Barb felt her keen observations made living more pleasurable.
              v   b   b   v
 13 She overcooked the bacon when broiling it in the oven.
          v   b   b   v b   b   v   v
 14 Vernon baked batches of biscuits with strawberry preserves and clove.
          v   b   v   b
 15 Alleviate burdens through decisive and responsible action.
              v   b   b   v
 16 An adventurous spirit can make one become appreciably more alive.
          b v   b   b   v   b
 17 Brevity is admirable, commendable, and effective in debates.
          b b   v   v   v   b   b
 18 Bob was conservative and competitive, albeit humble.
                v   v   v   b   b
 19 The conversation covered definitive strategies for balancing the budget.
          b   b   b   v   v   b
 20 The blossoms blew about in the vigorous evening breeze.

Phrases: *v* vs. *w*

AUDIO

7.6

Listen to the recording of the following phrases, then read the phrases aloud. Concentrate on distinguishing between the v and w sounds, which are marked phonetically.

    w   v
 1 requires valor

    w   v
 2 always forgiving

3 grieving widow

4 productive networking

5 quirky relative

6 voted to switch

7 a winding driveway

8 twelve warriors

9 native language

10 navigating the aquarium

11 disapproved of the quarrel

12 elusive acquaintance

13 wispy white sleeves

14 offensive Twitter

15 selective questions

16 loves winter weather

17 welcomes creative work

18 equally competitive

19 wonderful advice

20 vehemently inquisitive

Sentences: *v* vs. *w*

Listen to the recording of the following sentences, then read the sentences aloud. Concentrate on distinguishing between the v and w sounds, which are marked phonetically.

     v   w   w   v   w   v
1 Valerie wondered whether the renovation plans would be improved.

    w   v   w   v   v
2 She was relieved to qualify for and receive an advance.

    w   w   v   w v   v
3 Distinguish between convenient equivocation and real indecisiveness.

    w v   v v   w   w   w   v
4 Darwin voiced a theory of evolution, which was widely received.

    w   w   v   w   v   v
5 We'll quietly delve into questions before evaluating the controversy.

          w   w   v   v w   v
6 Is there frequently an equal division of work in the development

       v
division?

    w   v w   w   v   v   v   v
7 Wherever one looks in the aquarium, diverse varieties of fish thrive.

    w   w   w   v   v   v
8 Quality walking at quick intervals vitalizes vascular health.

    w   v   v   v   w   w
9 Which version of your verse do you want to tweak?

      v   v   w   v   v   w
10 The travel advisory warned the visitors of high winds.

    v   v   w   w   w v   v
11 Vin deserves a wage increase when waiving overtime pay.

      v   v   w   w   w v   v
12 You've been vague about which week you want vacation leave.

    w   v   w   w   v   v
13 Witty advertising awards were viewed on television.

       v w   v   v   v   w   w   w   w
14 If delivery were never available, everyone would wonder why.

       v   v   v   v   w w   v   v
15 The driver of the vehicle avoided the wet widths of the pavement.

16   Victor thought quality was always advisable over quantity.

17   The waitress at the sidewalk café strives to deliver quick service.

18   Be assertive and avid in your quest to acquire equipment.

19   Think conservatively whenever reviewing which assets to liquidate.

20   Unwise and convoluted conversations can twist language.

EIGHT

The consonant *j* or *g* (ʤ)

The ʤ sound defined

The consonant *j* or soft *g,* represented by the phonetic symbol ʤ, is frequently mispronounced by nonnative speakers of English, since it is confused with the consonant ʒ, as in the word *pleasure.* These sounds are very similar, but with an important distinction in placement. The second element of ʤ is, indeed, ʒ, but it is preceded by the consonant d. Physiologically speaking, the tongue touches the alveolar ridge (to form a d) before pulling back into the ʒ sound.

Step 1: Feeling the placement of ʤ

VIDEO

12

Turn now to **Video Track 12,** where a step-by-step demonstration of the placement of ʤ is presented. After you have watched the video, read the following description of the sound placement and do the exercises below.

Take out your mirror. Let's examine the position of the tongue in forming the consonant ʤ. Looking in the mirror, place the tip of your tongue against your lower teeth, with your tongue resting flat on the floor of your mouth.

First, we'll form the ʒ sound, since you can form this sound correctly. Say ʒ. Notice that the sides of your tongue are touching the inside of your upper teeth and that the tip of your tongue is pointed toward the alveolar ridge, but not touching it. Say ʒ . . . *massage.*

Next, we'll form the ʤ sound. Raise the tip of your tongue, place it against the alveolar ridge, and say d. Move your tongue backward slightly and feel the sides of your tongue touching the inside of your upper teeth, as you say ʒ. Now, form these two sounds sequentially. Start with the tip of your tongue on the alveolar ridge (for d), then move it slightly backward (for ʒ). Say d . . . ʒ . . . d . . . ʒ.

Finally, we'll combine d and ʒ. Place the tip of your tongue against the alveolar ridge, and pull your tongue backward during the production of the sound. Say ʤ . . . *age*.

Return now to **Video Track 12**. Practice the correct placement of the consonant ʤ.

Step 2: Hearing the placement of ʤ

Using the mirror, look closely inside your mouth. Place the tip of your tongue against your lower teeth, raise your tongue, and say ʒ. Notice that the sides of your tongue are touching the inside of your upper teeth and that the tip of your tongue is pointed toward the alveolar ridge. Say ʒ. You will hear this sound as long; it will continue as long as your vocal folds are vibrating.

Now, touch the tip of your tongue to the alveolar ridge, form a d sound, then move your tongue slightly backward into ʒ. Combining the two, say ʤ. Listen to the sound produced. This phoneme is much shorter than ʒ, since it is the result of the pressure from the first element (d) releasing into the second element (ʒ).

Watch in the mirror as you pronounce the pairs of words in the list below. Listen to the sound differences as well, so that you can train your ear to hear the distinction, as well as feel the physiological difference in placement.

ʒ	ʤ
sei<u>z</u>ure	sie<u>g</u>e
trea<u>s</u>ure	tru<u>dg</u>e
lu<u>x</u>urious	lun<u>g</u>e
massa<u>g</u>e	messa<u>g</u>e ▶

◄

ʒ	ʤ
pleasure	pledge
genre	gentle
casual	cage
illusion	imagine
lesion	legion
beige	badge

AUDIO

8.1

*Turn now to **Audio Track 8.1**,* which features the sound adjustments between ʒ and ʤ. Repeat the pairs of words, while comparing your pronunciation with that on the recording.

Record your own pronunciation, and compare it to the audio track. Repeat this exercise until you feel ready to proceed to the next step.

Step 3: Applying the placement of ʤ

Following are lists of common English words that contain the ʤ sound. You can practice this sound by checking your pronunciation against the word list recordings. After you have mastered the sound, advance to the phrases. Then move on to the sentences

AUDIO

8.2

INITIAL ʤ

gem	geology	gyroscope
gender	geometry	jab
gene	geranium	jack
general	germ	jacket
generation	gerund	jade
generic	gestate	jagged
generous	gesture	jail
genesis	giant	jam
genetic	gigantic	jangle
genial	gin	janitor
genie	ginger	January
genius	ginseng	Japan
gentle	giraffe	jar
genuflect	gym	jargon
genuine	gypsy	jaundice
geography	gyrate	jaunt

►

INITIAL ʤ (CONTINUED)

◄

jaw	joint	juice
jay	jolly	July
jealous	jolt	jumble
jeer	jostle	jump
jelly	jot	junction
jerk	journal	June
jest	journey	jungle
jet	jovial	junior
jiggle	joy	junk
jingle	jubilant	jury
jinx	judge	just
job	judgment	justice
jockey	jug	justification
jog	juggle	juvenile
join	jugular	juxtapose

MEDIAL ʤ

-ology (suffix)	angina	conjure
abject	anthology	contingent
abjure	anthropology	cordial
adjacent	apologize	curmudgeon
adjective	archeology	danger
adjoin	astringent	degenerate
adjourn	astrology	deject
adjudicate	badger	digestion
adjunct	belligerent	digit
adjust	budget	diligent
agency	cajole	dramaturgy
agenda	carcinogen	drudgery
agile	cogent	dungeon
agitate	cogitate	ecology
algae	congeal	education
algebra	congenial	egregious
allegiance	congest	eject
allergy	conjecture	eligible
analogy	conjugate	energy
androgynous	conjunction	engender
angel	conjuncture	engine

►

◄
enjoy	legend	prodigy
eulogy	legislate	project
evangelical	legitimate	refugee
exaggerate	lethargy	regiment
fidget	liturgy	region
fledgling	logic	register
fragile	longitude	reject
fraudulent	magenta	rejoice
frigid	magic	rejuvenate
fugitive	magistrate	religion
gadget	major	rigid
gorgeous	majority	scavenger
gradual	margarine	schedule
graduation	margin	sergeant
harbinger	misogynist	sojourn
homogenous	modulate	soldier
hydrangea	negligence	stingy
hydrogen	nitrogen	strategy
hygiene	objection	subject
illegible	objective	suggest
imagination	original	surgeon
immunology	oxygen	tangerine
incorrigible	pageant	tangible
indigenous	pajamas	tragedy
ingest	passenger	trajectory
inject	pejorative	vegetable
injunction	perjure	vegetarian
injure	photogenic	vengeance
interject	plagiarism	vigil
laryngitis	prejudice	vigilant
ledger	procedure	Virginia

FINAL ʤ

advantage	avenge	bridge
age	average	budge
allege	baggage	bulge
arrange	bandage	cabbage
assemblage	begrudge	cage
assuage	besiege	carnage

►

FINAL ʤ (*CONTINUED*)

◄ carriage

carriage	image	sage
cartilage	impinge	salvage
cartridge	indulge	sausage
centrifuge	infringe	savage
challenge	knowledge	scourge
change	large	scrimmage
charge	ledge	scrounge
college	lodge	sewage
converge	lounge	siege
cottage	lozenge	singe
cringe	lunge	sledge
damage	mange	sludge
derange	marriage	smudge
disparage	merge	splurge
diverge	message	stage
divulge	mortgage	storage
dodge	nudge	strange
dosage	oblige	submerge
dredge	orange	surge
edge	page	teenage
emerge	partridge	tinge
engage	patronage	trudge
estrange	pilgrimage	tutelage
foliage	pillage	twinge
forage	pledge	umbrage
forge	plunge	urge
fringe	privilege	usage
fudge	purge	verbiage
garbage	rage	verge
gauge	rampage	vestige
hedge	range	village
hemorrhage	ravage	vintage
heritage	revenge	voyage
hinge	ridge	wage
homage	rummage	wedge
hostage	sacrilege	wreckage
huge		

Phrases: dʒ

AUDIO
8.3

Listen to the recording of the following phrases, then read the phrases aloud. Concentrate on correctly pronouncing the dʒ sound, which is marked phonetically.

 1 enjoyed vegetable juice

 2 degenerate judge

 3 a gigantic gesture

 4 huge jar of jam

 5 legitimate advantage

 6 prejudiced the jury

 7 the gentle janitor

 8 dejected soldier

 9 original objective adjusted

10 a jacket in January

11 genuinely religious

12 photogenic in magenta

13 diligent surgeon

14 registered for algebra

15 a generation of refugees

16 dangerous journey

17 subjected to garbage

18 logical strategy

19 cordial in July

20 ingesting ginger jelly

Sentences: ʤ

AUDIO
8.4

Listen to the recording of the following sentences, then read the sentences aloud. Concentrate on correctly pronouncing the ʤ sound, which is marked phonetically.

1 Can we adjust the June and July budget on the project?

2 Jill spilled vegetable juice all over her magenta jacket.

3 Our joint agendas addressed both gender and generational subjects.

4 She diligently jotted down notes in her journal throughout the journey.

5 James judged the jargon to be juvenile and objectionable.

6 In January, Gina joined a gym near her job.

7 I was agitated by his negligence and lack of imaginative strategy.

8 Will you study immunology, anthropology, or archaeology in college?

9 The majority must be educated about energy usage and ecology.

10 What is the age range and average wage of the hedge funds' managers?

11 Is this page legitimately original, or was it plagiarized?

12 Don't bring charged and damaging emotional baggage to a marriage.

13 Would you prefer the dru͟dgery of a curmu͟dgeon or the dan͟ger

of a de͟generate?

14 He rummag͟ed through the ruins and salvag͟ed the le͟dgers from the

wreckag͟e.

15 John felt re͟juvenated by the jo͟vial and conge͟nial passen͟gers.

16 Jennifer's disparag͟ing remark had a damag͟ing effect on the ju͟ry.

17 The ser͟geant enjo͟yed geo͟logy, geo͟graphy, ge͟ometry, and al͟gebra.

18 My aller͟gic reaction to the foliag͟e verg͟ed on laryn͟gitis.

19 Is ju͟stice always obje͟ctive, lo͟gical, and ge͟nuine?

20 Jeremiah obje͟cted to proce͟dure based on conje͟cture and demanded

an apolo͟gy.

Phrases: dʒ vs. ʒ

Listen to the recording of the following phrases, then read the phrases aloud. Concentrate on distinguishing between the dʒ and ʒ sounds, which are marked phonetically.

AUDIO 8.5

1 a gen͟tle mas͟sage

2 plea͟sure in imagi͟nation

3 bei͟ge paja͟mas

4 trea͟sure in the jun͟gle

5 a lux͟urious jour͟ney

6 jolted by a seizure
   (dʒ)   (ʒ)

7 casual gym joiner
   (ʒ)   (dʒ) (dʒ)

8 major visual challenge
   (dʒ) (ʒ)   (dʒ)

9 usual liturgy
   (ʒ)   (dʒ)

10 measured more than average
    (ʒ)   (dʒ)

11 junk in the garage
    (dʒ)   (ʒ)

12 abject displeasure
    (dʒ)   (ʒ)

13 camouflaged jacket
    (ʒ)   (dʒ)

14 legendary espionage
    (dʒ)   (ʒ)

15 visually impaired passenger
    (ʒ)   (dʒ)

16 treasured his education
    (ʒ)   (dʒ)

17 pleasure in danger
    (ʒ)   (dʒ)

18 occasionally jaded
    (ʒ)   (dʒ)

19 legitimate conclusion
    (dʒ)   (ʒ)

20 envisioning a change
    (ʒ)   (dʒ)

Sentences: dʒ vs. ʒ

AUDIO
8.6

Listen to the recording of the following sentences, then read the sentences aloud. Concentrate on distinguishing between the dʒ and ʒ sounds, which are marked phonetically.

1 It's a pleasure to digest an argument that is logical and cogent.
         (ʒ)   (dʒ)   (dʒ)   (dʒ)

2 Who can measure the damage of an egregious error?

3 After the seizure, the surgeon's vision gradually worsened.

4 Take advantage of leisure time, and indulge lethargic impulses.

5 I treasure an ability to visualize challenge as pleasurable.

6 Is the dress code at the lodge's lounge usually casual?

7 Georgia's teenage protégé was a genius and a joy to teach.

8 Occasionally, Jen exaggerated her knowledge of a subject.

9 The merger gave the illusion that they had forged a prestigious new agency.

10 Jasper thought that the sale of the loft was contingent on persuasion through badgering.

11 Splurge on a massage and a luxurious, but energizing, range of activities.

12 The sergeant had his soldiers wear camouflage during the siege.

13 Joining forces involved collusion with fraudulent measures.

14 Take advantage of the festival and enjoy your favorite film genre.

15 Madge's teenagers usually felt obliged to accompany her on religious outings.

16 I take umbrage at Jessica's urge to feign prestige through excessive verbiage.

17 The vintage clothing line included gorgeous rouge lingerie and treasured jewelry.

18 I envisioned that my mortgage rate would surge and tried to adjust my budget.

19 You can sabotage your energy by eating carcinogens while on a hectic schedule.

20 Allusions to eligible singles abounded in the graduate student's journal.

NINE

The vowel ɪ

Fred was excited: He had been flown into New York City to interview for a highly coveted position at a large securities firm. During the taxi ride from the airport, he saw the city in its dizzying splendor—from skyscrapers to street vendors. Fred could picture himself living here as a true New Yorker, and he wanted to convey that to his potential boss. As he shook the CEO's hand, he announced passionately, "I want to leave here! Now!" The CEO was confused . . .

The ɪ sound defined

For nonnative speakers of English, the short *i* sound, represented by the phonetic symbol ɪ (as in *him*), is often confused with the vowel i (as in *he*). This is an understandable mistake, since i is used by nearly all languages and ɪ is used almost exclusively by English. These two different vowel sounds are made very close to each other, but with a definite difference in tongue placement.

Both i and ɪ are front vowels: The tip of the tongue is resting against the lower teeth and it is the arch in the front of the tongue that determines the vowels' sounds. The difference in the arch is minuscule—about one-eighth of an inch.

Correcting the i vs. ɪ vowel substitution is easy, once you learn the difference in tongue placement. It is also easy to recognize which of the two is used, based on the spelling patterns of each vowel.

The easily recognized i sound in English is spelled with *e, ea, ee, ei,* and *ie,* as in the words *be, eat, see, receive,* and *chief.* Final *y* in English words use the i sound, as in *happy* and *country.* The ɪ sound is almost always spelled with *i,* as in the words *in, with,* and *his,* or with medial *y,* as in *myth* and *syllable.*

Since most languages other than English pronounce *i* as i, its pronunciation as ɪ may be unfamiliar to you. As we saw in the unfortunate story above, Fred pronounced *live* as if it were *leave.* Similarly, you may think *is* is pronounced as *ease,* and *sit* as *seat,* but this is incorrect.

Step 1: Feeling the placement of ɪ

VIDEO

13

Turn now to **Video Track 13**, where a step-by-step demonstration of the difference between i and ɪ is presented. After you have watched the video, read the following description of the sound placement and do the exercises below.

Take out your mirror. Begin by saying the i sound, since you already pronounce this sound correctly. Say the word *he* several times. Looking in the mirror, become aware of your tongue's placement. Notice that the tip of your tongue is resting against your lower teeth and that the front of your tongue is arched forward. You can check yourself by placing the tip of your little finger on the top edge of your lower teeth, as demonstrated on the video. Feel the arch in the front of your tongue as it contacts your finger when you say *he.*

Return your tongue to its resting position, with the tip of your tongue against your lower teeth, but with the body of your tongue lying flat on the floor of your mouth. Say the word *he* again, freezing on the vowel. Once again, you will feel the arch of your tongue contact the tip of your finger.

Now, drop the arch of your tongue backward about one-eighth of an inch, leaving the tip of your tongue against your lower teeth. This is the placement of the vowel ɪ, as in the word *him.* Go back and forth between these two placements: i . . . ɪ . . . i . . . ɪ.

Return now to **Video Track 13**. Practice the difference in placement between the sounds i and ɪ.

Step 2: Hearing the placement of ɪ

Using the mirror, look closely inside your mouth. Move your tongue back and forth between the placements of these two words: *he ... him ... he ... him ... he ... him ... he ... him.* (Of course, your lips will come together for the consonant m.)

Watch in the mirror as you pronounce the pairs of words in the following list. Listen to the differences between i and ɪ, so that you can train your ear to hear the distinction, as well as feel the physiological difference in placement.

i	ɪ
be	bit
peel	pill
seat	sit
tea	tin
keep	king
meal	mill
eat	it
cheap	chip
these	this
reap	rip
feel	fill
heat	hit
feet	fit
key	kill
neat	knit

AUDIO

9.1

Turn now to **Audio Track 9.1**, which features the sound adjustments between i and ɪ. Repeat the pairs of words, while comparing your pronunciation with that on the recording.

Record your own pronunciation, and compare it to the audio track. Repeat this exercise until you feel ready to proceed to the next step.

Step 3: Applying the placement of ɪ

Following are lists of common English words that contain the ɪ vowel. You can practice this sound by checking your pronunciation against the word list recordings. After you have mastered the sound, advance to the phrases. Then move on to the sentences.

AUDIO

9.2

ɪ IN ONE-SYLLABLE WORDS

-ing (*suffix*)	gift	miss
mis- (*prefix*)	give	mist
been	grim	mix
bid	grin	pick
big	grip	pill
bills	guilt	pin
bit	hill	pink
brick	him	pit
bridge	hip	pitch
bring	his	prince
brisk	hit	print
build	if	quick
chill	ill	quit
chin	in	ribs
chip	inch	rich
did	is	rid
dip	it	ring
dish	kid	rip
disk	kill	risk
drill	king	script
drink	kiss	ship
drip	lick	sick
fifth	lid	sin
fig	lift	since
fill	limb	sink
film	lint	sing
fish	lip	sit
fist	list	six
fit	live (*verb*)	skill
fix	milk	skin
flip	mill	slid

►

◄

slim	strip	tip
slip	swift	trim
split	swim	trip
spill	swing	which
spring	switch	whip
squid	thick	will
stick	thin	win
stiff	thing	wind (*noun*)
still	think	wing
sting	this	wish
strict	till	wit
string	tin	with

ɪ IN TWO-SYLLABLE WORDS

acting	brilliant	cleaning
active	bringing	clinic
adding	British	closing
admit	building	clothing
artist	burning	coming
asking	business†	conflict
assist	bustling	consists
basic	busy	convict
basis	buying	convince
bearing	cabin	cooking
begin*	calling	cooling
being	captive	cousin
Berlin	ceiling	credit
bigger	changing	crisis
billboard	charming	critic
billing	chicken	crossing
billion	children	cutting
binding	Christmas	dealing
bitter	chronic	didn't
bizarre	city	dinner
breaking	civil	direct
breathing	classic	discharge

►

*This word has the letter *e* in an unstressed first syllable; the *e* is pronounced ɪ.
†This word has the letter *e* in a suffix; the *e* is pronounced ɪ (see Appendix A).

I IN TWO-SYLLABLE WORDS (*CONTINUED*)

◄

disease	fifteen	hearing
disgusts	fifty	heating
display	fighting	helping
distance	figure	himself
distinct	filthy	hither
district	finger	hitting
disturb	finish	holding
divine	firing	hoping
divorce	fiscal	horrid
doctrine	fishing	hospice
doing	fitting	hunting
drawing	flicker	ignore
dressing	fluid	image†
dripping	flying	impact
driven	forbid	imposed
drying	foreign	impress
during	forgive	improve
dying	forming	impulse
earnings	friendship	inclined
eating	fulfill	include
edit	furnish	income
ending	getting	increase
engine	giddy	indeed
English	giving	index
ethics	glitter	indoors
exist*	going	infer
exit	granite	inflict
fabric	graphic	inform
facing	growing	injure
falling	guilty	inner
famine	guitar	input
feeding	habit	insects
feeling	having	inside
fiction	heading	insight

►

---

*This word has the letter *e* in an unstressed first syllable; the *e* is pronounced ɪ.
†This word has the letter *a* in a suffix; the *a* is pronounced ɪ (see Appendix A).

◄ insist
inspired
install
instance
instead
insult
insure
intense
interest*
intern
into
intrigue
invent
invest
invite
involve
isn't
issue
itself
jaundice
justice
keeping
kidding
kindle
kingdom
kitchen
knowing
lacking
landing
languish
laughing
leading
learning
leaving
letting
lighting

limit
linen
liquid
liquor
listen
little
liver
livid
living
looking
losing
lying
magic
making
margin
massive
matching
meaning
meeting
melting
merit
middle
midnight
midtown
million
minute
mirror
mischief
missing
mission
mistake
misty
mixture
morning
motive
moving

mister/Mr.
missus/Mrs.
muffin
music
native
nibble
nothing
notice
office
painting
panic
parking
passing
paving
permit
persist
pickle
picnic
picture
pigeon
pillow
pistol
pitcher
pittance
pity
placing
planning
plastic
playing
pointing
portrait
practice
predict
pressing
pretty
prison ►

*This word has the letter *e* in a common word ending; the *e* is pronounced ɪ (see Appendix A).

I IN TWO-SYLLABLE WORDS (*CONTINUED*)

◀ privy | service | striking
profit | serving | struggling
promise | setting | stupid
public | shaking | submit
publish | sharing | swimming
pulling | shining | tactic
putting | shopping | taking
quickly | showing | talking
racing | signal | teaching
raising | silly | telling
ranging | silver | testing
rapid | simple | therein
reaching | singing | thinking
reading | single | thinner
resist* | sister | tissue
riding | sitting | tonic
rigid | sixty | tourist
rigor | skipping | toxic
risen | slimming | trading
river | slipper | traffic
ruin | smiling | tragic
ruling | solid | training
running | something | tranquil
sailing | sorting | transmit
sampling | Spanish | tribute
sandwich | speaking | tricky
saving | spending | trigger
scissors | spirit | triple
searching | splendid | tripping
seeing | splinter | trying
seeking | staring | tunic
selfish | starting | turning
selling | sticky | unit
sending | stingy | until ▶

---

*This word has the letter *e* in an unstressed first syllable; the *e* is pronounced ɪ (see Appendix A).

◄ using   waiting   window
valid   walking   winner
vicious   warning   winter
victim   washing   wisdom
vigor   watching   wishing
villa   wearing   within
villains   wedding   without
vision   wherein   women
visit   whisper   working
vivid   whistle   worship
voting   widow   written

I IN WORDS OF THREE OR MORE SYLLABLES

ability   aspirin   clarity
arbitrator   assistant   classical
academic   Atlantic   classification
accident   atomic   clinical
accomplish   attitude   coincidence
activity   attractive   collective
addition   attribute   combination
administration   audition   commission
admission   authentic   commitment
aesthetic   authority   committee
Africa   authorization   commodity
agriculture   automatic   communication
alternative   availability   community
ambiguous   beautiful   comparison
ambition   benefit   competition
American   biological   complicate
amicable   capability   compliment
animal   capacity   composition
anniversary   capital   condition
anticipate   certify   confidence
antidote   characteristic   conservative
application   charity   consider
architecture   chemical   consistent
article   citizen   Constitution
artificial   civilization   contaminate
artistic   clarification   contingence ►

I IN WORDS OF THREE OR MORE SYLLABLES (CONTINUED)

◄
continue	disaster	fellowship
contradict	discipline	festival
contribution	discontent	forbidden
conviction	discover	fortify
cooperative	discriminate	frivolous
counterfeit	discussion	fugitive
creative	disinfect	furniture
credible	disorganization	genuine
criminal	displacement	heroic
critical	disposal	hesitate
criticism	disposition	hidden
decision*	dispute	hideous
dedicate	distinction	historical
definition	distribution	history
definitive*	division	holiday
delicatessen	domestic	horrible
delicious*	dominant	hospital
deliver*	dramatic	hostility
democratic	dynamic	humanity
density	economic	humidifier
derision*	emphasis	identify
despicable*	episode	identity
destiny	epitaph	idiot
determination*	equipment*	ignorant
dictionary	ethical	illusion
difference	evidence	illustration
different	examine*	imagination
difficult	executive*	imitation
dignity	exhibit*	immature
dilemma	experiment*	immigrant
diligent	extraordinary*	immortal
dimension	facility	impatient
diplomatic	familiar	impeccable
direction	family	impediment
director	fantastic	impending
disappear	favorite	implication	►

*These words have the letter *e* in an unstressed first syllable; the *e* is pronounced I (see Appendix A).

◄ important
impossible
impression
incident
incisive
incredible
independent
indicate
indigestion
indirect
indispensable
individual
industry
inevitable
infection
infinite
inflammation
influence
information
ingredient
inherent
inhibit
initial
initiative
innocent
insertion
insolence
inspection
institution
instruction
instrument
insufficient
insurance
integration
intellectual
intelligence
intensity

intention
interference
interior
intermission
intermittent
internal
international
interpretation
interrupt
interval
intervention
interview
intimidate
introduce
invariably
invention
investigation
investment
invisible
irritate
jurisdiction
justify
leadership
legislation
liberty
limitation
linear
literally
literature
logical
magnetic
magnificent
majority
manipulate
mathematical
maturity
maximum

mechanical*
medicine
membership
metabolism*
metropolitan
military
milligram
minimal
minister
minority
miserable
mislead
monitor
morality
multiple
musical
narrative
negative
nutrition
obituary
objective
obligation
obliterate
oblivious
official
opinion
opportunity
opposite
optimum
ordinary
organic
organization
original
Pacific
participation
particular
peripheral ►

---

*These words have the letter *e* in an unstressed first syllable; the *e* is pronounced ɪ (see Appendix A).

I IN WORDS OF THREE OR MORE SYLLABLES *(CONTINUED)*

◄   permission

personality

perspective

pertinent

philosophy

pinnacle

pitiful

plausible

policy

politics

position

positive

possibility

practical

precision*

preliminary*

president

primarily

primitive

principle

prisoner

privilege

probability

productive

prognosis

prominent

prospective

provision

publication

publicity

purify

quality

quantity

radical

rapidly

realistic

reality

realization

recognition

refrigeration*

register

rehabilitation

relationship*

relative

religion*

representative

residence

residual*

responsibility*

ridiculous

ritual

romantic

sacrifice

satisfactory

scholarship

scientific

security*

seductive*

sensitive

significance

similar

situation

socialism

specialist

specific*

stabilization

statistic

stimulate

strategic

substitute

sufficient

superficial

supervision

suspicion

technical

television

temporarily

terrible

terrify

territory

testimony

theoretical

tradition

transition

trivial

uniform

unity

universal

university

utility

vanilla

vehicle

velocity*

victory

video

vigorous

violin

visible

visitor

visual

vitality

Washington

---

*These words have the letter *e* in an unstressed first syllable; the *e* is pronounced
ɪ (see Appendix A).

I WITH y SPELLING IN ONE-SYLLABLE WORDS

crypt	hymn	myth
cyst	lymph	nymph
gym	lynch	tryst

I WITH y SPELLING IN TWO-SYLLABLE WORDS

Brooklyn	lyric	synapse
cryptic	mystic	syndrome
cymbal	physics	syntax
cynic	rhythm	syringe
crystal	symbol	syrup
gypsy	symptom	system

I WITH y SPELLING IN WORDS OF THREE OR MORE SYLLABLES

analysis	idiosyncrasy	symbolism
anonymous	myriad	sympathy
chrysanthemum	mystery	symphony
cylinder	Olympics	synagogue
dysfunction	oxygen	synchronize
glycerin	physical	syndicate
homonym	physician	synonym
hypnosis	pyramid	typical
hypocrisy	syllable	tyranny
hysterical	symbolic	

Note: The -ing suffix always uses the vowel ɪ.

Phrases: ɪ

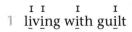

AUDIO

9.3

Listen to the recording of the following phrases, then read the phrases aloud. Concentrate on correctly pronouncing the ɪ sound, which is marked phonetically.

    ɪ ɪ   ɪ   ɪ
1 living with guilt

         ɪ   ɪ
2 charming prince

3 begins to think

4 upcoming conflict

5 children spilled milk

6 script analysis

7 sick of pills

8 convincing pitch

9 Phil's slick grin

10 built six ships

11 trimmed the thin tunic

12 beginning to drill

13 washing the dishes

14 chronic sickness

15 insight in the morning

16 permission to quit

17 bigger billboard

18 sink or swim

19 active in the gym

20 cooking a delicious dinner

AUDIO
9.4

Sentences: ɪ

Listen to the recording of the following sentences, then read the sentences aloud. Concentrate on correctly pronouncing the ɪ sound, which is marked phonetically.

1 Jill's physical condition will influence an impending accident.

2 Bill introduced a combination of video images and still pictures.

3 It was a disaster when the drink spilled all over the clinical evidence.

4 The office had a policy of nondiscrimination for women.

5 She rapidly fingered the guitar strings, producing beautiful music.

6 The intern examined Mr. Miller's hip and indicated a positive prognosis.

7 The administration stressed the importance of interviews to the six candidates.

8 In my opinion, physical activity is important.

9 I wish the script had been less typical and better written.

10 The menu consists mainly of squid and is quite limited.

11 I initially take aspirin when I practice my English.

12 Cindy's chronically bad vision caused her to make many mistakes at the university.

13 Chris resisted building in a traditional and unimaginative architectural style.

14 I imagine a plausible situation in which Bill's interests and intelligence are utilized.

15 It is silly to begin dinner when Phil is still missing.

16 In the middle of the disaster, the thought of a tranquil dip in the Pacific
was calming.

17 The authorities sought the evidence to convict the convict in the
vicious assault.

18 We think Tim should reconsider the situation and admit to his guilt.

19 His inability to sit still compromised his willingness to finish the
project.

20 My little sister is persistent in interfering in my business.

Phrases: ɪ vs. i

Listen to the recording of the following phrases, then read the phrases
aloud. Concentrate on distinguishing between the ɪ and i sounds, which
are marked phonetically.

1 a brisk chilling breeze

2 risky business

3 he's a convict

4 a little bit of heat

5 drinking cheap whisky

6 feeling like eating

7 easy to miss him

      ɪ ɪ i   i

8 this city street

      ɪ ɪ   i

9 assisting Neil

      ɪ ɪ   i

10 a critical achievement

      ɪ ɪ   i   ɪ

11 singing sheet music

      ɪ   ɪ   i

12 whispering thief

      i ɪ   ɪ ɪ

13 bleeding victim

      ɪ   i

14 promise to meet

      i ɪ   ɪ ɪ

15 scenic rushing river

      i   ɪ   ɪ i

16 breathing with ease

      i   i   i ɪ i

17 seems really picky

      ɪ i   i ɪ   i

18 pristine cleaning machine

      ɪ ɪ   i

19 a minute to dream

      i   ɪ   ɪ i

20 streaming video

Sentences: ɪ vs. i

AUDIO

9.6

Listen to the recording of the following sentences, then read the sentences aloud. Concentrate on distinguishing between the ɪ and i sounds, which are marked phonetically.

      i ɪ ɪ   ɪ i   ɪ   ɪ ɪ ɪ ɪɪ   i   ɪ   i

1 He insists his seemingly insignificant deed was a victory and

      i

  an achievement.

2 Christie feels she's completely fulfilled her obligation in a meaningful way.

3 She dreams of having a sleek, discreet, and impeccably clean condo by the sea.

4 The insight of the team leader inspired the artistic productivity of all.

5 We agreed instantly that his team's mistakes created the disastrous conflict.

6 Lee needed clarification before proceeding, as the instructions were misleading.

7 Responsible people can complete a key project with impressive precision.

8 Sheila's metabolism increased with brisk walking and additional protein.

9 Keep believing that consistent practice leads to dramatic improvement.

10 His esteemed intelligence gives credibility to his unusual system of working.

11 Deep breathing increases circulation and improves vitality.

12 Is Tim satisfied with the quality of the steam machine?

13 Gina picked a tin of pickled beets to bring on the picnic.

14 Did you eat the beef sandwiches I was saving for dinner?

15 Teaching can frequently seem difficult, but it's rewarding.

16 The thief will keep stealing until he is apprehended.

   ɪ ɪ   ɪ   ɪ ɪ   i i   i   i   ɪ   ɪ

17 Nick is quick-witted, genial, and completely motivated.

       ɪ ɪ i   ɪ i   iɪ   ɪ   ɪ   ɪ   ɪ i   ɪ   i

18 I definitely believe being determined and ambitious will lead to victory.

        ɪ   ɪ i   i   i ɪ   i

19 The festive city streets were appealing to Jean.

  i i   i   ɪi ɪ   ɪ   i

20 He seized the opportunity to interrupt the bizarre procedure.

For more details about the use of the vowel ɪ in prefixes and suffixes with unusual spelling patterns, see Appendix A.

TEN

The vowel *e*

The *e* sound defined

The short *e* sound, represented by the phonetic symbol e (as in *hem*), is a potential pronunciation problem for nonnative speakers of English. The *e* spelling pattern is used in other languages, but it is usually pronounced more openly, as ε, which is not used in English. The ε pronunciation is often substituted for the more closed e used by English. These two different vowel sounds are made very close to each other, but with a definite difference in tongue placement.

Like ɪ, which we discussed in the previous chapter, e is a front vowel: For both sounds, the tip of the tongue rests against the lower teeth and it is the arch in the front of the tongue that determines the phoneme. The difference in the arch is minuscule—about one-eighth of an inch between the two. The e vowel is usually spelled with *e*; it is also used in the suffix *-ary* (as in *secretary* and *ordinary*), as well as in the words *any* and *many*.

Step 1: Feeling the placement of *e*

*Turn now to **Video Track 14**,* where a step-by-step demonstration of the placement of e, in contrast to the placement of i and ɪ, is presented. After you have watched the video, read the following description of the sound placement and do the exercises below.

VIDEO

14

Take out your mirror. Begin by saying the i sound. Say the word *he* several times. Looking in the mirror, check the placement of your tongue. Notice that the tip of your tongue is resting against your lower teeth and that the front of your tongue is arched forward. You can check yourself by placing the tip of your little finger on the top edge of your lower teeth, as demonstrated on the video exercise. Feel the arch in the front of your tongue as it contacts your finger when you say *he*.

Drop the arch in the front of your tongue back about one-eighth of an inch, leaving the tip of your tongue against your lower teeth. This is the placement of the vowel ɪ, as described in the previous chapter. Say i...*he*...ɪ...*him*.

Now, drop the arch in the front of your tongue back about an additional one-eighth of an inch. This is e...*hem*. Say these three front vowels as you feel the arch in the front of your tongue drop back about one-eighth of an inch for the next phoneme: i...ɪ...e...*he*...*him*...*hem*.

Return now to **Video Track 14**. Practice the difference in placement among the vowels i, ɪ, and e.

Step 2: Hearing the placement of e

Using the mirror, look closely inside your mouth. Move your tongue back and forth between the placements of these three words: *he, him, hem* ...*he, him, hem*...*he, him, hem*. (Of course, your lips will come together for the consonant m.)

Watch in the mirror as you pronounce the pairs of words in the following list. Listen to the differences between ɛ and e, so that you can train your ear to hear the distinction, as well as feel the physiological difference in placement.

Note: In previous chapters (except Chapter Five), the sound placement for each new phoneme was contrasted with that of another, frequently substituted phoneme. However, since no words in English use ɛ, the words in the list are the same in both columns. The purpose of the exercise is to pronounce each word incorrectly with ɛ, then correctly with e. The difference between the two is recorded on Audio Track 10.1.

ɛ (INCORRECT)	e (CORRECT)
b<u>e</u>t	b<u>e</u>t
c<u>e</u>nt	c<u>e</u>nt
fr<u>e</u>sh	fr<u>e</u>sh
g<u>e</u>t	g<u>e</u>t
m<u>e</u>lt	m<u>e</u>lt
n<u>e</u>xt	n<u>e</u>xt
pl<u>e</u>dge	pl<u>e</u>dge
th<u>e</u>n	th<u>e</u>n
r<u>e</u>nt	r<u>e</u>nt
f<u>e</u>ll	f<u>e</u>ll
th<u>e</u>m	th<u>e</u>m
m<u>a</u>ny	m<u>a</u>ny
fr<u>e</u>t	fr<u>e</u>t
wh<u>e</u>n	wh<u>e</u>n
y<u>e</u>s	y<u>e</u>s

AUDIO
10.1

Turn now to **Audio Track 10.1,** which features the sound adjustments between ɛ and e. Repeat the pairs of words, while comparing your pronunciation with that on the recording.

Record your own pronunciation, and compare it to the audio track. Repeat this exercise until you feel ready to proceed to the next step.

Step 3: Applying the placement of *e*

Following are lists of common English words that contain the e vowel. You can practice this sound by checking your pronunciation against the word list recordings. After you have mastered the sound, advance to the phrases. Then move on to the sentences.

AUDIO
10.2

e IN ONE-SYLLABLE WORDS

b<u>e</u>d	b<u>e</u>lt	b<u>e</u>st
b<u>e</u>g	b<u>e</u>nch	b<u>e</u>t
b<u>e</u>ll	b<u>e</u>nt	bl<u>e</u>nd ►

e IN ONE-SYLLABLE WORDS (*CONTINUED*)

◄

bless	fresh	realm
bread	fret	red
breast	friend	rent
breath	get	rep
bred	guess	rest
cell	guest	said
cent	head	self
check	health	sell
chef	held	send
chess	hell	sense
chest	help	shed
clench	hem	shelf
crept	hen	shell
crest	jet	shred
dead	kept	sketch
deaf	led	sled
debt*	left	smell
deck	lend	sped
delve	lens	spell
den	less	spend
dense	meant	stem
dent	melt	step
depth	men	strength
desk	met	stress
dread	neck	stretch
dress	nest	swell
dwell	next	tempt
edge	peg	ten
else	pen	tend
end	pest	tent
fed	pet	test
fell	pledge	text
fence	press	them
fled	quench	then
flesh	quest	thread

►

---

*The *b* in this word is silent and not pronounced.

◄ threat   web   when

tread   well   wreck

trend   went   wrench

vent   wept   yes

vest   west   yet

vet   wet   zest

Certain spelling patterns with *e* in a prefix or suffix are pronounced as ɪ, and therefore not underlined in the next two lists. See Appendix A for details.

e IN TWO-SYLLABLE WORDS

-ary (*suffix*)	central	defect
accent	chemist	defend
accept	cherish	deflect
address	cherry	deject
adept	clever	dentist
again	collect	depend
against	commence	detect
amend	commend	detest
any	comment	devil
ascend	compel	digest
aspect	complex	divest
assess	compress	echo
assets	concept	edit
attempt	condense	effect
attend	confess	effort
attest	congest	elect
avenge	connect	empty
belly	contempt	engine
berry	content	enter
better	contest	entrance
bisect	context	envy
breakfast	convent	errand
bury	credit	error
cadet	crescent	essay
cement	crevice	ethics
censure	debit	ethnic
center	decade	event ►

e IN TWO-SYLLABLE WORDS (*CONTINUED*)

◄

ever	lemon	rebel
excerpt	length	record (*noun*)
exhale	letter	reflect
expect	level	reflex
expend	many	regret
expense	measure	repress
expert	member	rescue
express	mental	respect
extend	mention	revenge
extra	menu	second
feather	merit	section
ferry	message	segment
forget	metal	seldom
freckle	method	select
frenzy	neglect	sentence
gender	nephew	separate
gentle	never	session
gesture	pebble	seven
heaven	peddle	shelter
heavy	penny	shepherd
hectic	pension	sheriff
helmet	pepper	skeptic
immense	peril	special
impend	perish	spectrum
impress	pleasure	success
indent	plenty	suggest
index	precious	suppress
inept	preface	suspect
inflect	premise	suspend
intend	present (*noun, adjective*)	temper
intense	pressure	tempo
invest	pretend	tender
jealous	prevent	tennis
kettle	project	tenor
leather	protest	tension
lecture	question	terrace
legend	ready	terror

►

◄ treasure

tremble

trespass

unless

upset

velvet

vendor

venue

very

vessel

weather

wedding

welcome

welfare

whether

wrestle

yellow

zealous

e IN WORDS OF THREE OR MORE SYLLABLES

accelerate

accessible

accessory

addendum

adventure

aesthetic

affection

agenda

aggression

America

ancestor

anesthetize

antiseptic

apathetic

appendix

apprehend

apprehension

architect

assemble

attention

benefit

beverage

burial

calisthenics

celebrate

celebrity

celery

celestial

cellophane

cemetery

century

cessation

clientele

comprehend

conception

condescend

confection

conjecture

consecutive

consequence

contemporary

correction

credible

crescendo

deception

decorate

dedicate

deficit

definite

delicate

demonstrate

deposition

deprecate

designate

desperate

destiny

devastate

develop

dialect

dictionary

dilemma

dimension

direction

discrepancy

disinfect

dispensable

disseminate

domestic

eccentric

edible

educate

election

electric

elegant

element

elephant

elevate

eleven

embezzle

emerald

empathy

emulate

enemy

energy

entity

equity

especially ►

e IN WORDS OF THREE OR MORE SYLLABLES (*CONTINUED*)

◄ essential

estimate

everything

evidence

evolution

excellent

excessive

execute

exercise

experiment

extrovert

February

feminine

festival

fiduciary

flexible

general

generation

generous

genuine

heritage

hesitate

identity

impeccable

incentive

infection

inherit

intelligent

jeopardize

legacy

legislation

medical

melody

memory

mesmerize

metaphor

necessary

negative

objective

pedigree

penalty

percentage

phonetic

predicate

prejudice

preparation

presentation

president

pretentious

profession

progression

propensity

reception

recession

recipe

recognition

recommend

reconcile

rectify

reference

reflexive

register

regular

remember

renovate

repetition

reprehensible

reputation

retrospect

revenue

reverence

secretary

sedentary

seminar

sentiment

separate

September

serendipity

severance

specify

speculate

subjective

supremacy

surrender

susceptible

telephone

television

temperature

temporary

territory

testify

therapy

together

umbrella

utensil

vegetable

verify

yesterday

Phrases: *e*

AUDIO
🎧
10.3

Listen to the recording of the following phrases, then read the phrases aloud. Concentrate on correctly pronouncing the e sound, which is marked phonetically.

1   my best friend

2   a very fresh scent

3   chest congestion

4   fell on her entrance

5   tempted the guest

6   commendable quest

7   envied Ken's effort

8   dejected elephant

9   precious element

10   apprehended the suspect

11   suspended development

12   healthy stress test

13   adept at accents

14   ethically correct

15   event of the decade

16   breakfast in bed

17   expensive architect

      e   e
18 presenting a medal

    e   e   e
19 kept left of the fence

  e   e
20 ending the reception

Sentences: e

*Turn to **Audio Track 10.4**. Listen to the recording of the following sentences, then read the sentences aloud. Concentrate on correctly pronouncing the e sound, which is marked phonetically.

AUDIO
10.4

     e   e   e   e   e   e
1 In retrospect, I recognize the merits of the intense seminar.

     e   e   e   e   e   e
2 Against better judgment, Erin commenced the event with a lecture

     e
on health.

     e   e   e e   e
3 When under stress, you should stretch, rest, and exercise.

        e   e   e   e   e   e
4 Did Ken's letter mention that he spent Wednesday with my best

     e
friend?

     e   e   e   e
5 The expert expressed an immense desire to win the contest.

         e   e   e   e   e
6 Are you compelled to attend a session on the trends of bank lending?

     e   e   e   e   e
7 When can Jerry collect his well-earned pension?

        e   e   e   e
8 In the hectic frenzy, the more minor errands were neglected.

       e   e   e   e   e
9 The protesters outside the tent were met with threatening gestures.

    e   e e   e e   e
10 Members of the press speculated about the presidential election.

11 Did you ever expect the heavy pressure to divest your assets?

12 I guessed that Ted fretted and vented when faced with an error.

13 Ethically, can Evan try to get a "yes" from every guest?

14 Did you intend for your clever comment to be taken out of context?

15 Measure the ingredients before attempting any estimate to a recipe.

16 He recommended ending a devastating debt through temporary but select credit.

17 Discrepancy in the project's professional preparation could have jeopardizing effects.

18 I suggest avoiding regrets when delving into the past.

19 The melody was mesmerizing, especially as it accelerated toward the crescendo.

20 The chef's impeccable presentation kept the menu fresh and the clientele dedicated.

ELEVEN

The vowel æ

The æ sound defined

The short *a* sound, represented by the phonetic symbol æ (as in *ham*), is often mispronounced by nonnative speakers of English. Depending on a person's native language, the vowel æ can be pronounced too tightly, like ɛ, or too openly, like ɑ.

Like e, which was discussed in the previous chapter, æ is a front vowel: For both sounds, the tip of the tongue rests against the lower teeth and it is the arch in the front of the tongue that determines the phoneme. The difference in the arch is minuscule—about one-eighth of an inch between the two. The æ vowel is always spelled with *a*.

Step 1: Feeling the placement of æ

VIDEO

15

Turn now to **Video Track 15**, where a step-by-step demonstration of the placement of æ, in contrast to the placement of i, ɪ, and e, is presented. After you have watched the video, read the following description of the sound placement and do the exercises below.

Take out your mirror. Begin by saying the i sound. Then say the word *he* several times. Looking in the mirror, check the placement of your tongue. Notice that the tip of your tongue is resting against your lower teeth and that the front of your tongue is arched forward. You can check yourself by placing the tip of your little finger on the top edge of your lower teeth, as demonstrated on the video exercise. Feel the arch in the front of your tongue as it contacts your finger when you say *he*.

Drop the arch in the front of your tongue back about one-eighth of an inch, leaving the tip of your tongue against your lower teeth. This is the placement of the vowel ɪ. Now, drop the arch in the front of your tongue back about an additional one-eighth of an inch, as described in the previous chapter. This is e. Say these first three front vowels as you feel the arch in the front of your tongue drop back about one-eighth of an inch for the next phoneme: i . . . ɪ . . . e . . . *he . . . him . . . hem*.

Now, drop the arch in the front of your tongue back about an additional one-eighth of an inch. This is æ . . . *ham*. Say all four front vowels as you feel the arch in the front of your tongue drop back about one-eighth of an inch for the next phoneme: i . . . ɪ . . . e . . . æ . . . *he . . . him . . . hem . . . ham*.

Now that you've located the placement of æ, let's contrast æ with ɑ. As demonstrated on the video, put your little finger back in your mouth and say æ. Then, drop your tongue flat onto the floor of your mouth. This is ɑ. Go back and forth between the two placements: æ . . . ɑ . . . æ . . . ɑ . . . æ . . . ɑ.

Return now to **Video Track 15**. Practice the difference in placement among the vowels i, ɪ, e, and æ, as well as the physical contrast between æ and ɑ.

Step 2: Hearing the placement of æ

Using the mirror, look closely inside your mouth. Move your tongue back and forth between the placements of these four words: *he, him, hem, ham . . . he, him, hem, ham . . . he, him, hem, ham*. (Of course, your lips will come together for the consonant m.)

Watch in the mirror as you pronounce the pairs of words in the following list. Listen to the vowel sound changes, so that you can train your ear to hear the distinction, as well as feel the physiological difference in placement.

e	æ
bet	bat
beg	bag
set	sat
flesh	flash
guess	gas
neck	knack*
mess	mass
pen	pan
ten	tan
wreck*	rack
lend	land
men	man
send	sand
bend	band
vet	vat

AUDIO

11.1

*Turn now to **Audio Track 11.1**,* which features the sound adjustments between e and æ. Repeat the pairs of words, while comparing your pronunciation with that on the recording.

Record your own pronunciation, and compare it to the audio track. Repeat this exercise until you feel ready to proceed to the next step.

Step 3: Applying the placement of æ

Following are lists of common English words that contain the æ vowel. In addition, there is an "answer" list, which contains common words where an *a* spelling is pronounced with ɑ in British English, but with æ in American English. You can practice the æ sound by checking your pronunciation against the word list recordings. After you have mastered the sound, advance to the phrases. Then move on to the sentences.

---

*When the *kn* or *wr* spelling pattern occurs at the beginning of a syllable or word, the *k* or *w* is silent and not pronounced.

æ IN ONE-SYLLABLE WORDS

act	clang	jazz
add	clap	knack
and	clash	lab
ash	crab	lack
at	crack	lag
ax	cramp	lamb
back	crank	lamp
bad	crash	land
badge	crass	lapse
bag	dad	lash
ban	damp	mad
band	dash	man
bang	drab	map
bank	drag	mass
bash	fact	mat
bat	fan	match
batch	fax	math
blab	flag	nag
black	flap	nap
bland	flash	pack
blank	flat	pact
brag	frank	pad
bran	gag	pal
brand	gang	pan
brat	gap	pants
cab	gas	patch
camp	glad	plaid
can	grab	plan
cap	grand	prank
cash	hack	rack
cat	ham	rag
catch	hand	ran
chap	hang	ranch
chat	hat	rang
clad	hatch	rank
clam	hath	rash
clamp	have	rat
clan	jam	sack

►

◄
sad	snag	thank
sag	snap	that
sand	span	track
sang	spasm	tramp
sat	stab	trance
scalp	stack	trap
scrap	staff	trash
scratch	stamp	valve
shack	stand	van
shall	strand	vat
slab	strap	wag
slack	tack	wax
slam	tag	wrap
slang	tan	wrath
slap	tap	yank
smash	task	
snack	tax	

æ IN TWO-SYLLABLE WORDS

abbey	angle	attack
absent	angry	attic
abstract	anguish	attract
accent	ankle	avid
acid	annex	baffle
active	anti	balance
actress	antique	ballet
adapt	antler	ballot
addict (*noun*)	anxious	bandit
adverb	apple	banish
agile	arid	banner
alas	arrow	banquet
album	ashes	banter
alley	asset	barrel
aloe	asthma	barren
amber	astral	battle
ambush	atlas	began
ample	atom	bladder
anchor	attached	blanket

►

æ IN TWO-SYLLABLE WORDS (*CONTINUED*)

◄

bracket	compact	haddock
brandy	contact	hadn't
cabbage	contract	hammer
cactus	cracker	hamper
caffeine	dagger	handle
camel	damage	happen
campus	dandruff	happy
canal	dangle	hasn't
cancel	dazzle	haven't
candid	detach	havoc
candle	detract	hazard
candor	dispatch	impact
candy	distract	intact
canon	drastic	jacket
canteen	exact	jagged
canyon	exam	lackey
capsule	expand	ladder
captain	fabric	language
caption	facile	Latin
captive	factor	latter
carrot	fancy	madam
carry	fashion	magic
cascade	finance	malice
cashew	flashlight	manage
cashmere	flatter	manic
catcher	fraction	mansion
cattle	fragile	married
cavern	fragment	matter
challenge	frantic	narrow
champagne	gadget	package
channel	gallon	packet
chapel	gamble	pamper
chapter	garish	panel
chatter	gather	panic
clamor	glamour	passion
clatter	grammar	passive
climax	grapple	pattern
collapse	habit	perhaps

►

◄ phantom
planet
plastic
practice
protract
rabbit
racket
ramble
rampant
random
rapid
rattle
relax
romance
salad
salmon
salvage
sample
sanction
sandwich
satire
scaffold
scandal

scramble
shadow
shampoo
slander
Spanish
sparrow
spasm
stagger
stagnant
standard
static
statue
status
stature
strangle
subtract
tackle
tactic
talent
tamper
tango
tatter
traffic

tranquil
transcend
transcribe
transcript
transfer
transform
transfused
transit
translate
transmit
transpire
transverse
travel
vaccine
vacuum
valid
valiant
valley
vanish
vapid
wagon

æ IN WORDS OF THREE OR MORE SYLLABLES

abandon
abdicate
abdomen
abnormal
absolute
abstinence
academy
accident
accurate
accusation
acquisition
acrobat
actual

adamant
adequate
adjective
admirable
admiral
adolescence
adoration
adversary
advertise
advocate
affable
affidavit
affirmation

affluent
Africa
aggravate
agitate
agony
agriculture
alcohol
alfalfa
algebra
alibi
alkaline
allegation
allergy ►

æ IN WORDS OF THREE OR MORE SYLLABLES (*CONTINUED*)

◄ alligator
allocate
alphabet
altitude
altruism
alveolar
amalgam
amateur
ambassador
ambiguous
ambulance
amicable
amnesty
amorous
amplify
amputate
anagram
analogy
analysis
ancestor
anecdote
animal
animate
anniversary
annual
antagonism
anticipate
antidote
antiseptic
anxiety
apparent
appetite
application
apprehend
aptitude
arrogance
aspirate
aspirin

asterisk
astronaut
atmosphere
atrophy
attitude
attribute (*noun*)
avarice
avenue
average
bachelor
bacteria
balcony
banana
bandana
baptism
barricade
brutality
cabaret
cafeteria
calcium
calculate
calendar
caliber
calisthenics
calorie
camouflage
candidate
canopy
cantaloupe
capital
caravan
casserole
castigate
casually
catalyst
catastrophe
category
caterpillar

catholic
cavalcade
cavalry
cavity
ceramic
champion
chandelier
character
chariot
charitable
charity
circumstance
clarify
collaborate
companion
comparison
congratulate
contaminate
dialysis
diameter
diaphragm
diplomat
distraction
dramatic
dynamic
elaborate
elastic
embarrass
erratic
evacuate
evaluation
evaporate
exacerbate
exact
exaggerate
examine
exasperate
extraction ►

◄ extravagant
fabulous
faculty
family
fantastic
fascination
financial
galaxy
gallery
gasoline
gigantic
gradually
graduate
gratitude
gravity
guarantee
handicap
hospitality
humanity
imagine
infallible
international
January
laboratory
laminate
lateral
magazine

magnify
majesty
management
manager
mandatory
manifest
mannequin
manual
manufacture
masculine
masterpiece
matrimony
morality
mortality
national
natural
palatable
palpable
palpitate
paradise
parallel
parody
piano
practical
pragmatic
ramification
ratify

rationalize
reaction
retraction
sacrifice
sanctity
sanitary
sanity
satisfaction
Saturday
spectacular
stamina
strategy
substantial
tangible
tantalize
tragedy
transaction
transcription
transition
transportation
understand
vacillate
valuable
vernacular
vitality
vocabulary

THE "ANSWER" LIST: æ IN ONE-SYLLABLE WORDS

ask	brass	chance
bask	calf*	chant
bath	calve*	clasp
blanch	can't	class
blast	cask	craft
branch	cast	dance ►

*When the *alf* or *alv* spelling pattern occurs at the end of a syllable or word, the *l* is silent and not pronounced.

THE "ANSWER" LIST: æ IN ONE-SYLLABLE WORDS (*CONTINUED*)

◄

draft	half*	raft
fast	halve*	rasp
flask	lance	shaft
France	last	slant
gasp	laugh	staff
glance	mask	task
glass	mast	trance
graft	pass	vast
grant	past	wrath
graph	path	
grasp	plant	
grass	prance	

THE "ANSWER" LIST: æ IN TWO-SYLLABLE WORDS

advance	enchant	pasture
after	enhance	plaster
alas	fasten	rascal
answer	forecast	rather
basket	ghastly	sample
behalf	giraffe	slander
casket	lather	transplant†
castle	master	trespass
command	nasty	vantage
demand	pastor	

THE "ANSWER" LIST: æ IN WORDS OF THREE OR MORE SYLLABLES

advantage	disaster	raspberry
avalanche†	example	reprimand
chancellor	flabbergast†	telegraph
disadvantage	paragraph†	

---

*When the *alf* or *alv* spelling pattern occurs at the end of a syllable or word, the *l* is silent and not pronounced.

†In these words, both *a* spellings are pronounced æ in American English. In British English, the first *a* is pronounced æ and the second is pronounced ɑ.

Phrases: æ

Listen to the recording of the following phrases, then read the phrases aloud. Concentrate on correctly pronouncing the æ sound, which is marked phonetically.

AUDIO
11.3

    æ   æ æ
1 asking in advance

     æ   æ
2 glad to nap

     æ   æ   æ
3 handed Jack cash

     æ   æ
4 damp blanket

    æ   æ
5 bank balance

    æ   æ
6 barren land

     æ   æ
7 attractive package

     æ   æ
8 random spasm

     æ   æ
9 relaxing in cashmere

     æ   æ
10 half a sandwich

     æ   æ
11 narrow passageway

     æ   æ
12 panicked but passive

      æ   æ
13 the agony of traffic

     æ   æ
14 abandoned affluence

   æ   æ
15 anticipate analysis

Sentences: æ

AUDIO
🎧
11.4

Listen to the recording of the following sentences, then read the sentences aloud. Concentrate on correctly pronouncing the æ sound, which is marked phonetically.

1. Mandy is a talented actress who admires the impact of transformative theater.

2. Looking back, Max was glad he had not made a pact and signed a contract.

3. Before the banquet, we served crackers, cheese, clams, and champagne.

4. Sandy managed to translate the classic transcript into four languages.

5. He's planning on transferring a substantial number of credits for his bachelor's degree.

6. Rather than advocating collaboration, the candidates seemed ambiguous.

7. It takes stamina to manifest desires into tangible matter.

8. Frankly, I prefer answering my phone to texting; I like human contact.

9. Are you satisfied with your manager's pragmatic evaluation process?

10. Chad added tango melodies to his jazz band's practice.

11. Pack cantaloupe and mango sorbet in the picnic basket.

12. Jan planned on wearing plaid pants to match her travel bag.

13. He allocated little cash for his travel in France.

     æ   æ   æ   æ

14 A dis<u>a</u>strous <u>a</u>ccident was prevented by l<u>a</u>st-minute ev<u>a</u>cuation.

       æ   æ   æ   æ

15 It was <u>a</u>nguishing to watch how <u>a</u>rrogant the <u>a</u>mateur <u>a</u>cted.

Phrases: æ vs. e

Listen to the recording of the following phrases, then read the phrases aloud. Concentrate on distinguishing between the æ and e sounds, which are marked phonetically.

AUDIO
11.5

       æ   e
1 h<u>a</u>ppy <u>e</u>nding

          e   æ   e
2 the ch<u>e</u>f's r<u>a</u>nch dr<u>e</u>ssing

      æ   e
3 attr<u>a</u>ctive inv<u>e</u>stment

      e   æ
4 b<u>e</u>nding the br<u>a</u>nch

      e   æ   æ   æ
5 t<u>e</u>n t<u>a</u>nned <u>a</u>crob<u>a</u>ts

      e   æ
6 <u>e</u>nergized but <u>a</u>nxious

      e   æ
7 r<u>e</u>cipe for dis<u>a</u>ster

      æ   e
8 a t<u>a</u>x cr<u>e</u>dit

      æ   e
9 att<u>a</u>cking his prof<u>e</u>ssion

       e   æ
10 exp<u>e</u>cting an <u>a</u>nswer

       e   æ   e
11 sugg<u>e</u>sted st<u>a</u>ggering sch<u>e</u>dules

       e   e   æ   æ
12 r<u>e</u>comm<u>e</u>nded cont<u>a</u>cting <u>A</u>lice

       e   æ   æ
13 s<u>e</u>nding a n<u>a</u>rrow p<u>a</u>ckage

```
        e    e        æ
14  the secretary's vocabulary

        e       æ        e
15  members passed the agenda
```

Sentences: æ vs. e

AUDIO
11.6

Listen to the recording of the following sentences, then read the sentences aloud. Concentrate on distinguishing between the æ and e sounds which are marked phonetically.,

```
     e        æ        e        e      e        æ  e    e  æ         æ
1  Fred was apprehensive when addressing his accent, yet tackled practice

        æ
   with vitality.

     æ   æ          æ                  æ        æ        e
2  Advancing in status within the bank's branch depended on

      e              e
   demonstrating credibility.

        æ          e      e    e                        e
3  Some answers will present themselves through quieting excessive

      e       æ
   mental chatter.

        æ          æ           e        e      æ
4  The advocate abandoned his reflexively pretentious mask.

        æ        æ        e      e   æ          æ
5  The accident aggravated Ben's intense abdominal cramps.

     æ      æ   æ  æ          e           æ         e
6  Acting crassly and arrogantly seldom commands respect.

          e              æ   e      æ     æ      æ  æ
7  What serendipity to transcend both grandstanding and actively

      æ         e
   slandering reputations!

        e        æ              æ   æ         æ   æ
8  The weather forecaster predicted damp afternoons and patchy fog

      æ      e    e
   patterns in February.
```

  æ   e   æ   æ   e   e
9 The plan to disseminate Anne's financial records was unpleasant

  e e
but necessary.

  æ   e æ   e æ   e
10 Does altitude affect attitude when traveling domestically?

  e   æ   e æ   æ   æ
11 The tennis match between Eric and Matthew was challenging.

  æ   e   æ   æ   e   æ
12 Caffeine is a mood elevator, but can have the negative impact of

     æ
causing anxiety.

  æ   e   æ   e   æ
13 Can you comprehend the baffling concept, or is it too protracted

  æ   e
and inaccessible?

  æ   æ   e   e   æ
14 Andrew's apparent sense of supremacy made him appear arrogant

  æ   e
and condescending.

  æ   æ   æ   e   e e
15 Maggie worked absolute magic in the editing room, yet everything

     e
seemed effortless.

Phrases: æ vs. ɑ

AUDIO

11.7

Listen to the recording of the following phrases, then read the phrases aloud. Concentrate on distinguishing between the æ and ɑ sounds, which are marked phonetically.

  æ   ɑ
1 demanded pasta

  ɑ   æ
2 calm in traffic

  ɑ   æ
3 father was adamant

æ   ɑ
4 acted pompous

æ æ   ɑ
5 an antique clock

æ   ɑ   æ
6 at the bottom of the class

    æ   ɑ æ
7 attacked in combat

   ɑ   æ
8 qualified applicant

   ɑ   æ
9 contradicted Pam

ɑ   æ
10 operating the camp

  ɑ   æ
11 fond of ballet

æ   ɑ
12 matching socks

æ   ɑ æ
13 bragged about his contract

æ   ɑ
14 dynamic drama

æ   ɑ
15 lacking confidence

Sentences: æ vs. ɑ

AUDIO
11.8

Listen to the recording of the following sentences, then read the sentences aloud. Concentrate on distinguishing between the æ and ɑ sounds, which are marked phonetically.

æ   æ   æ   ɑ   ɑ
1 Jan was happily distracted by watching espionage films.

æ   æ ɑ ɑ   æ
2 The anniversary celebration happened on a balmy afternoon

ɑ
in Washington.

   æ   æ   ɑ   ɑ   æ   ɑ

3 Dashing Angelo was a suave renaissance man with both bravado

   æ   æ

and laughter.

         æ   ɑ   æ   æ   æ æ   æ

4 The romantic aria was enchanting and created an amorous atmosphere.

   æ æ   æ   æ   ɑ   ɑ

5 Can accurate and specific information be camouflaged in nuance?

   æ   æ   æ   ɑ   ɑ   ɑ

6 After cranking out the massive project, I deserved a calming massage.

               ɑ   æ   æ   ɑ ɑ æ   æ æ

7 Would you prefer a pasta casserole, or a salad with avocado and alfalfa
sprouts?

         ɑ   ɑ   æ   ɑ   æ   æ

8 For a finale, the soprano sang Rodgers and Hammerstein's "Shall We

   æ

Dance?"

   æ   æ   æ æ

9 Examples of English alphabet spelling can't accurately explain the

   ɑ

schwa phoneme.

   æ   ɑ   ɑ   ɑ   æ   æ

10 Adding palm trees to the façade of the spa enhanced the relaxing

   ɑ   ɑ

ambience.

               ɑ   æ   æ   æ   æ

11 They called "Bravo!" after the amateur cabaret's climax.

      æ   æ   ɑ   ɑ   æ æ

12 Unimaginable circumstances made Father feel swamped and agitated

   æ

by his calendar.

   ɑ   ɑ   ɑ   ɑ   æ

13 Macho police squad dramas are depicted on national television.

   æ   ɑ   æ   ɑ   æ

14 Brad qualified to compete in the black belt karate match.

              æ   æ   ɑ   ɑ   ɑ

15 Which would you rather magnify—a product's quantity or its quality?

TWELVE

The vowels of *r* (ɝ and ɚ)

The ɝ/ɚ sounds defined

The vowels of *r*, represented by the phonetic symbols ɝ (in a stressed syllable) and ɚ (in an unstressed syllable) are frequently mispronounced by nonnative speakers of English. Depending on your native language, you may pronounce the vowels of *r* too tightly, because of too much tension in the back of your tongue. Or the *r* coloring may be dropped, because the tip of your tongue is touching your lower teeth.

Step 1: Feeling the placement of ɝ/ɚ

VIDEO

16

Turn now to **Video Track 16**, where a step-by-step demonstration of the placement of the vowels ɝ/ɚ is presented. After you have watched the video, read the following description of the sound placement and do the exercises below.

These two *r* vowels are sounded the same; they have different phonetic representations because of the syllable stress within words (see Chapter Seventeen for a detailed explanation of syllable stress). Stressed syllables within words are enunciated with more emphasis and are typically longer, louder, and higher in pitch than unstressed syllables. The vowel ɝ is used in a stressed syllable within a word. The unstressed vowel ɚ marks a syllable as shorter and lower in pitch.

Take out your mirror. Let's examine the position of the tongue in forming the vowels ɝ/ɚ. Begin by placing the tip of your tongue against your lower teeth, with your tongue lying flat on the floor of your mouth. Now, lift only the tip of your tongue and say ɝ.

To produce the consonant r, the sides of your tongue touch the inside of your upper teeth and your tongue is lifted close to the alveolar ridge. By contrast, to pronounce the vowels of r, ɝ/ɚ, the tip of your tongue is lifted only slightly, no higher than the bottom of your upper teeth, and the sides of your tongue do not make contact anywhere inside your mouth.

The most difficult problem you will have with the ɝ/ɚ placement is a tendency toward tongue retraction. Because the tip of your tongue isn't touching anywhere inside your mouth, the back of your tongue may tense and pull backward to feel "anchored." As demonstrated on the video, place your thumb under your jaw at the base of your tongue. Hold your thumb there firmly as you lift only the tip of your tongue. This will prevent your tongue from retracting backward.

Return now to **Video Track 16.** Practice the placement of the vowels ɝ/ɚ.

Step 2: Hearing the placement of ɝ/ɚ

Using the mirror, look closely inside your mouth. Say ɝ . . . ɚ . . . ɝ . . . ɚ. Hear that the two vowels sound the same, except that ɝ has more emphasis and is longer and higher in pitch than ɚ. The examples of the words *hurt* (ɝ) and *other* (ɚ) demonstrate this. The tip of your tongue is lifted only slightly for both, no higher than the bottom of your upper teeth, and the sides of your tongue should not be touching anywhere inside your mouth.

Watch in the mirror as you pronounce the pairs of words in the following list. Listen to the vowel sound changes, so that you can train your ear to hear the distinction, as well as feel the physiological placement.

ɝ	ɚ
m<u>er</u>ger	merg<u>er</u>
m<u>ur</u>der	murd<u>er</u>
m<u>ur</u>mur	murm<u>ur</u>
n<u>ur</u>ture	nurt<u>ure</u>

▶

ɝ	ɚ
◄ purpose	paper
adverse	adversary
affirm	affirmation
circle	circulation
confer	conference
observe	observation
perfume (*noun*)	perfume (*verb*)
prefer	preference
survey (*noun*)	survey (*verb*)

AUDIO
12.1

*Turn now to **Audio Track 12.1**,* which features the pronunciation of ɝ and ɚ. Repeat the pairs of words, while comparing your pronunciation with that on the recording.

Record your own pronunciation, and compare it to the audio track. Repeat this exercise until you feel ready to proceed to the next step.

Note: The first four sets of words contain both the strong ɝ and ɚ vowels and are read only once on the recording.

Step 3: Applying the placement of ɝ/ɚ

Following are lists of common English words that contain the ɝ and ɚ sounds. You can practice the sounds by checking your pronunciation against the word list recordings. After you have mastered the sound, advance to the phrases. Then move on to the sentences.

AUDIO
12.2

ɝ IN ONE-SYLLABLE WORDS

birch	churn	earn
bird	clerk	earth
birth	curb	err
blur	curl	firm
blurb	curse	first
blurt	curt	flirt
burn	curve	fur
burst	dirge	girl
chirp	dirt	girth ►

ɝ IN ONE-SYLLABLE WORDS (*CONTINUED*)

◄

heard	search	turn
her	serve	urge
herb*	shirt	urn
herd	sir	verb
hurl	skirt	verge
hurt	smirk	verse
irk	splurge	were
jerk	spur	weren't
learn	spurn	whirl
lurk	spurt	word
mirth	stern	work
nurse	stir	world
pearl	surf	worm
per	surge	worse
perch	term	worst
perk	terse	worth
pert	third	yearn
purr	thirst	
purse	turf	

ɝ IN TWO-SYLLABLE WORDS

absurd	circus	curry
accursed	clergy	curtain
adjourn	coerce	curtsy
adverse	colonel†	desert (*verb*)
affirm	concern	deserve
alert	concur	dessert
assert	confer	deter
averse	confirm	discern
avert	converge	disperse
burlap	converse	disturb
certain	convert (*verb*)	diverge
circle	curfew	diverse
circuit	current	divert

►

---

*The *h* in *herb* is silent and not pronounced in American English.

†*Colonel* is the only English word that contains an r pronunciation but has no *r*.

◄ early   merchant   serpent
earnest   mercy   sturdy
emerge   merger   submerge
ergo   murder   superb
exert   murky   surcharge
fertile   murmur   surface
fervor   nurture   surgeon
flourish   observe   surplus
furbish   occur   survey (*noun*)
furnace   overt   thirty
furnish   perfect (*adjective*)   thorough
further   perfume (*noun*)   Thursday
furtive   person   transfer (*verb*)
gurgle   perturbed   turkey
hermit   prefer   turmoil
hurdle   purchase   turnip
hurry   purple   turquoise
immerse   purpose   turtle
infer   recur   urban
infirm   refer   usurp
insert (*verb*)   research (*verb*)   worry
journal   reserve   worship
journey   return

ɚ IN WORDS OF THREE OR MORE SYLLABLES

allergic   detergent   internal
alternative   determine   interpret
anniversary   deterrent   inversion
aspersion   disconcerted   maternal
attorney   discourage   nocturnal
aversion   eternal   paternal
certify   excursion   percolate
circulate   exterminate   perforate
circumstance   furniture   permanent
commercial   germinate   perpetrate
concerted   hernia   persecute
conservative   hurricane   pertinent
conversion   impertinence   refurbish
currency   impervious   rehearsal   ►

ɝ IN WORDS OF THREE OR MORE SYLLABLES (*CONTINUED*)

◄

resurgence	superlative	turbulence
reversal	surrogate	turpentine
suburban	terminate	
superfluous	thermostat	

ɚ IN TWO-SYLLABLE WORDS

-ar (*suffix*)	cellar	donor
-er (*suffix*)	censure	eager
-or (*suffix*)	center	effort
actor	chapter	ember
after	chatter	enter
altar	cider	error
alter	cipher	ever
amber	clatter	expert
anchor	clever	factor
anger	closure	falter
answer	cluster	farther
arbor	clutter	father
ardor	collar	favor
armor	color	feather
author	comfort	feature
awkward	concert (*noun*)	ferment
banner	conquer	figure
barter	cougar	filter
better	counter	finger
bicker	cover	fixture
bitter	cracker	flatter
blender	crater	flavor
blister	culture	flutter
blunder	curtail	forget
border	danger	forgive
brother	daughter	future
butcher	desert (*noun*)	gather
butter	differ	gender
camphor	dinner	gesture
candor	doctor	ginger
cater	dollar	glamour

►

◀ glimmer
glitter
grammar
hammer
hamper
hanger
harbor
hinder
honor
horror
humor
hunger
insert (*noun*)
intern
juncture
junior
juror
ladder
leader
leather
lecture
ledger
letter
limber
linger
litter
luster
manner
martyr
master
matter
meager
member
mentor
meter
minor
mixture
modern
moisture

molar
monster
mother
motor
mustard
nature
neither
never
odor
order
other
pamper
paper
partner
pasture
pattern
pepper
perfect (*verb*)
perform
perfume (*verb*)
perhaps
persist
persuade
pertain
picture
pillar
pitcher
plaster
platter
pleasure
poker
polar
ponder
posture
powder
power
pressure
proper
prosper

puncture
pursue
rather
razor
render
research (*noun*)
roster
rupture
sailor
scatter
scholar
scissors
sculpture
seizure
senior
shelter
shepherd
shoulder
shudder
shutter
silver
simmer
singer
sister
slander
slaughter
slender
smolder
smother
solar
soldier
spider
splatter
splendor
sponsor
stammer
stature
stranger
structure ▶

ɚ IN TWO-SYLLABLE WORDS (*CONTINUED*)

◄

stubborn	taper	timber
suffer	teacher	traitor
sugar	temper	transfer (*noun*)
summer	tender	treasure
super	tenure	trigger
surmise	terror	tutor
surprise	texture	ulcer
survey (*verb*)	theater	usher
tailor	thunder	utter
tamper	tiger	western

ɚ IN WORDS OF THREE OR MORE SYLLABLES

administrator	confirmation	intercede
adventure	consider	intercept
adversary	contractor	intermediate
advertise	contributor	intermission
advisor	conversation	international
affirmation	creditor	interview
altercation	customer	investor
alternate	December	jeopardize
alveolar	decipher	manufacture
amateur	deliver	meander
ambassador	departure	mediator
ancestor	diameter	mediocre
appetizer	director	messenger
asunder	disaster	minister
bachelor	employer	misdemeanor
benefactor	enamored	muscular
bifurcate	encounter	nuclear
calculator	energy	observation
calendar	engender	officer
carpenter	entertain	overture
character	exercise	particular
chiropractor	expenditure	passenger
circulation	exterior	peculiar
composure	familiar	percentage
conference	hibernate	perceptible

►

◄ perfunctory   professor   signature
   permission   property   similar
   perpetual   prosecutor   singular
   perspective   recover   sinister
   philosopher   register   spectacular
   photographer   regular   spectator
   popular   remember   surveillance
   posterior   repercussion   together
   predecessor   secular   ulterior
   preference   semester   vinegar
   procedure   September   yesterday

Phrases: ɝ vs. ɚ

Listen to the recording of the following phrases, then read the phrases aloud. Concentrate on correctly pronouncing the ɝ and ɚ sounds, which are marked phonetically.

AUDIO
12.3

1 mediocre clerk

2 the earth's energy

3 future earnings

4 daughter wants dessert

5 a purple banner

6 teacher answered firmly

7 hinders adversity

8 early favor

9 conferred about the merger

10 permission to curse

11 fli<u>r</u>ted with dan<u>ger</u>

12 pre<u>fer</u>red to w<u>or</u>k und<u>er</u> press<u>ure</u>

13 t<u>er</u>minated in Septemb<u>er</u>

14 anniv<u>er</u>sary yest<u>er</u>day

15 my sist<u>er</u>'s j<u>our</u>ney

16 des<u>er</u>ved to be spons<u>or</u>ed

17 p<u>er</u>manent mark<u>er</u>

18 makes a bett<u>er</u> w<u>or</u>ld

19 f<u>ur</u>th<u>er</u> meas<u>ure</u>s

20 a wond<u>er</u>ful exc<u>ur</u>sion

Sentences: ɝ vs. ɚ

Listen to the recording of the following sentences, then read the sentences aloud. Concentrate on the pronunciation of the ɝ and ɚ sounds, which are marked phonetically.

AUDIO
12.4

1 The ambassad<u>or</u> aff<u>ir</u>med clos<u>ure</u> on the bart<u>er</u>.

2 H<u>er</u>b<u>er</u>t had a p<u>er</u>ceptible av<u>er</u>sion to alt<u>er</u>cations.

3 Both act<u>or</u>s and sing<u>er</u>s p<u>er</u>formed with p<u>ur</u>pose at the gath<u>er</u>ing.

4 Pet<u>er</u>'s awkw<u>ar</u>d answ<u>er</u> conc<u>er</u>ned invest<u>or</u>s.

5 He was dist<u>ur</u>bed by c<u>er</u>tain <u>ur</u>ban od<u>or</u>s.

6 Do you p<u>er</u>ceive <u>ear</u>thy col<u>or</u>s to be p<u>ar</u>ticul<u>ar</u>ly comf<u>or</u>ting?

7 I'm perturbed by a surge in perfunctory performances in theater.

8 Laverne yearned for an energizing herbal dessert.

9 The intern immersed herself in further research.

10 Stay alert and discerning to avoid disasters.

11 Tickets to the popular circus can be purchased this Thursday.

12 I am eager to exercise in the refurbished modern gym.

13 Birds chirped as they perched on the corner of the arbor.

14 Did you confirm the dinner reservations on Saturday?

15 The scholar felt pressured to pursue worthy work.

16 Her allergic reaction to camphor triggered a fever.

17 Kirsten has two older sisters and a younger brother.

18 The leaders of yesterday's merger pledged a better use of power.

19 Do professors remember the days of registering for September semesters?

20 My cat Ferguson purrs with pleasure on sunny summer afternoons.

THIRTEEN

The vowel ʌ

The ʌ sound defined

The short *u* sound, represented by the phonetic symbol ʌ (as in *puddle*), is almost always mispronounced by nonnative speakers of English. It is usually replaced by the vowel ɑ (as in *pasta*). This is an understandable mistake, since ɑ is found in nearly all languages and ʌ is used almost exclusively in English. These two vowel sounds are made very close to each other, but with a definite change in the arch of the tongue from one to the other.

For both sounds, the tip of the tongue is resting against the lower teeth. But ʌ is a middle vowel, with a distinct arch in the middle of the tongue. By contrast, ɑ is a back vowel, occurring farther back in the mouth. In addition, ɑ is the only English vowel where the tongue has no arch but remains flat on the floor of the mouth.

Correcting the ʌ/ɑ vowel substitution can be easy, once one learns the difference in their tongue placements. It is also easy to recognize which of the two should be used by remembering a spelling pattern formula: ʌ is usually spelled with *u* (as in *bus, cup,* and *judge*) and sometimes with *o* (as in *mother, one,* and *love*), while ɑ is usually spelled with *o* (as in *honest, bond,* and *rock*), although there is a small number of words that are pronounced with ɑ and are spelled with *a* (as in *father, drama,* and *pasta*).

Let's pause for a moment and take a deep breath—this is not as confusing as it sounds. True, we have just entered the mysterious world of

169

the *o* spelling pattern, a shining example of the lack of logic in the correspondence between pronunciation and spelling in the English language. But there is a trick here that you can use to distinguish between ʌ and ɑ: Just look at the word lists in this chapter. All the common words in English that use an *o* spelling pattern and are pronounced with ʌ are found in the "ʌ with *o* spelling" lists in this chapter. If a word spelled with *o* is not on one of these lists, it is either pronounced with ɑ or with the diphthong oǒ, which is addressed in Chapter Sixteen. And all the common words in English that are pronounced with ʌ—either with an *o* or *u* spelling pattern—are in the word lists in this chapter.

Now, let's turn our attention to the difference in the physical placements of ʌ and ɑ.

Step 1: Feeling the placement of ʌ

VIDEO

17

Turn now to **Video Track 17**, where a step-by-step demonstration of the difference between ʌ and ɑ is presented. After you have watched the video, read the following description of the sound placements and do the exercises below.

Take out your mirror. Begin by saying ɑ, since you already pronounce this sound correctly. Say the word *ah* several times. Looking in the mirror, become aware of your tongue's placement. Notice that the tip of your tongue is resting against your lower teeth and the entire body of your tongue is lying flat on the floor of your mouth. You can check yourself by placing the tip of your little finger on the top edge of your lower teeth, as demonstrated on the video. Feel that there is no arch in your tongue against your finger as you say *ah*.

Now, keeping the tip of your tongue against your lower teeth, let the middle of your tongue arch forward about one-quarter inch against your finger. This is the placement of the vowel ʌ, as in *up*. Move back and forth between these two vowel positions: ɑ . . . ʌ . . . ɑ . . . ʌ.

Return now to **Video Track 17**. Practice the difference in placement between the sounds ʌ and ɑ.

Step 2: Hearing the placement of ʌ

Using the mirror, look closely inside your mouth. Move your tongue back and forth between the placements of these two words: *ah . . . up . . . ah . . . up . . . ah . . . up . . . ah . . . up.* (Of course, your lips will come together for the consonant p.)

Watch in the mirror as you pronounce the pairs of words in the following lists. Listen to the differences between ʌ and ɑ, so that you can train your ear to hear the distinction, as well as feel the physiological difference in placement.

ʌ WITH *u* SPELLING	ɑ WITH *a* SPELLING
f<u>u</u>n	f<u>a</u>ther
pl<u>u</u>g	p<u>a</u>sta
dr<u>u</u>m	dr<u>a</u>ma

ʌ WITH *u* SPELLING	ɑ WITH *o* SPELLING
b<u>u</u>t	b<u>o</u>tch
p<u>u</u>ff	p<u>o</u>llen
s<u>u</u>dden	s<u>o</u>ck
t<u>u</u>mble	T<u>o</u>m
cl<u>u</u>tch	cl<u>o</u>ck
ch<u>u</u>ckle	ch<u>o</u>p
th<u>u</u>nder	thr<u>o</u>ttle
r<u>u</u>b	r<u>o</u>b
h<u>u</u>t	h<u>o</u>t
p<u>u</u>n	p<u>o</u>nder
c<u>u</u>lture	c<u>o</u>lumn
n<u>u</u>t	n<u>o</u>t

ʌ WITH *o* SPELLING	ɑ WITH *o* SPELLING
m<u>o</u>ther	m<u>o</u>nster
br<u>o</u>ther	br<u>o</u>th
<u>o</u>ther	h<u>o</u>nest
fl<u>oo</u>d	f<u>o</u>nd
t<u>o</u>ngue	t<u>o</u>ngs

*Turn now to **Audio Track 13.1**,* which features the sound adjustments between ʌ and ɑ. Repeat the pairs of words, while comparing your pronunciation with that on the recording.

Record your own pronunciation, and compare it to the audio track. Repeat this exercise until you feel ready to proceed to the next step.

Step 3: Applying the placement of ʌ

Following are lists of common English words that contain the ʌ vowel. You can practice this sound by checking your pronunciation against the word list recordings. After you have mastered the sound, advance to the phrases. Then move on to the sentences.

ʌ WITH *o, oe, oo,* OR *ou* SPELLING IN ONE-SYLLABLE WORDS

blood	monk	son
come	month	sponge
does	none	ton
done	of	tongue
dove (*noun*)	once	touch
flood	one	tough*
from	rough*	won
front	shove	young
glove	slough*	
love	some	

ʌ WITH *o* OR *ou* SPELLING IN TWO-SYLLABLE WORDS

above	confront	enough*
affront	country	frontier
among	couple	govern
become	cousin	honey
beloved	cover	hover
brother	covet	income
color	doesn't	London
comfort	double	Monday
compass	dozen	money

►

*When the *gh* spelling pattern occurs at the end of a syllable or word, it is often pronounced f.

◄ monkey

mother

nothing

onion

other

outcome

oven

pommel

retouch

shovel

smother

somehow

someone

something

sometimes

somewhat

somewhere

southern

stomach

trouble

wonder

youngster

ʌ WITH O SPELLING IN WORDS OF THREE OR MORE SYLLABLES

accompanist

accompany

another

anyone

brotherhood

comfortable

comforter

company

coverage

discomfort

discover

everybody

everyone

governess

government

governor

nobody

otherwise

overcome

recover

slovenly

somebody

wonderful

wondrous

ʌ WITH U SPELLING IN ONE-SYLLABLE WORDS

bluff

blunt

blush

brunt

brush

brusque

buck

bud

budge

buff

bug

bulb

bulge

bulk

bum

bump

bun

bunch

bunk

bunt

bus

bust

but

butt

buzz

chuck

chunk

club

clump

clutch

crumb*

crunch

crush

crust

crutch

cub

cuff

cult

cup

cusp

cut

drug

drum

drunk

duck ►

---

*When the *mb* spelling pattern occurs at the end of a syllable or word, the *b* is silent and not pronounced.

Λ WITH *u* SPELLING IN ONE-SYLLABLE WORDS (*CONTINUED*)

◄

duct	hug	nub
dug	huh	nudge
dull	hulk	null
dumb*	hull	numb*
dump	hum	nun
dusk	hump	nut
dust	hunch	pluck
Dutch	hung	plug
fluff	hunk	plum
flung	hunt	plump
flunk	hush	plunge
flush	husk	plus
flux	hut	plush
fudge	judge	pub
fun	jug	puff
fund	jump	pulp
funk	junk	pulse
fuss	just	pump
fuzz	luck	pun
glum	lug	punch
glut	lull	punk
grudge	lump	punt
gruff	lunch	pup
grunt	lung	rub
gulf	lush	rug
gull	lust	rum
gulp	much	run
gum	mud	rung
gun	mug	runt
gush	mulch	rush
gust	mull	rust
gut	mumps	rut
hub	musk	scrub
huff	must	scruff

►

---

*When the *mb* spelling pattern occurs at the end of a syllable or word, the *b* is silent and not pronounced.

◄ scrunch   snug   sun
scuff   sprung   sung
sculpt   spud   sunk
scum   spun   swum
shrub   spunk   swung
shrug   struck   thrush
shrunk   strum   thrust
shun   strung   thud
shush   stub   thug
shut   stuck   thumb*
skull   stud   thump
skunk   stuff   thus
sludge   stump   truck
slug   stun   trunk
slum   stung   trust
slump   stunt   tub
slung   sub   tuck
slush   such   tug
smudge   suck   tusk
smug   sulk   up
snub   sum   us

ʌ WITH *u* SPELLING IN TWO-SYLLABLE WORDS

abrupt   buckle   chuckle
adjunct   buddy   clumsy
adult   budget   cluster
afflux   bundle   clutter
annul   bungle   conduct
begun   bunny   construct
blubber   bustle   consult
bludgeon   butler   corrupt
blunder   butter   crumble
bluster   button   culprit
bubble   buzzard   culture
bucket   chubby   cunning   ►

---

*When the *mb* spelling pattern occurs at the end of a syllable or word, the *b* is silent and not pronounced.

Λ WITH *u* SPELLING IN TWO-SYLLABLE WORDS (*CONTINUED*)

◄

custom	judgment	rubber
defunct	juggle	rubbish
discuss	jumble	rubble
disgust	jumbo	rudder
disrupt	junction	ruffle
distrust	juncture	rugby
divulge	jungle	rumble
duchess	justice	rummage
dulcet	knuckle	rumple
dungeon	kumquat	runner
erupt	lumber	rupture
expunge	luscious	Russia
exult	muddle	rustic
fluster	muffin	rustle
flutter	mumble	scrumptious
frustrate	muscle	scuffle
fumble	muslin	sculpture
function	mustache	scuttle
fungus	mustard	shudder
funnel	muster	shuffle
funny	mutter	shutter
grumble	number	shuttle
grumpy	nuzzle	slumber
gusto	obstruct	smuggle
gutter	occult	snuggle
huddle	plunder	sputter
Hudson	public	structure
humble	publish	struggle
hundred	puddle	stubble
hunger	pulsate	stubborn
hungry	pumpkin	study
hunter	pundit	stumble
husband	punish	subject (*noun*)
hustle	puppet	sublet
impulse	puzzle	substance
indulge	refund	substrate
influx	repulse	subtle
insult	result	suburb

►

◄

subway	supple	unction
suction	surplus	upgrade
sudden	suspect (*noun*)	uplift
suffer	thunder	upper
suffix	trumpet	upright
sulfate	truncate	uproar
sulfur	tumble	upset
sullen	tunnel	upside
sultry	tussle	upstairs
summer	ugly	uptown
summit	ulcer	upward
summon	ultra	utter
sundae	umbrage	vulgar
Sunday	umpire	vulture
sunny	uncle	
supper	under	

ʌ WITH *u* SPELLING IN WORDS OF THREE OR MORE SYLLABLES

abundance	custody	introduction
accustom	customer	jugular
adjustment	deduction	justification
agriculture	destruction	justify
assumption	difficult	luxury
asunder	discussion	multiple
autumnal	enunciate	mushroom
avuncular	exculpatory	nullification
befuddle	expulsion	nullify
buffalo	filibuster	penultimate
Columbia	fluctuate	percussion
combustible	fundamental	perfunctory
compulsion	gullible	production
compulsive	illustrious	productive
conductor	incumbent	profundity
conjunction	induction	pronunciation
construction	industrial	publication
consumption	industrious	publicity
cucumber	injunction	pulmonary
culminate	instruction	pulverize
cumbersome	interrupt	pumpernickel

►

∧ WITH *u* SPELLING IN WORDS OF THREE OR MORE SYLLABLES (*CONTINUED*)

◄ punctual

punctuate

punctuation

punishment

rambunctious

reduction

redundant

reluctance

renunciation

repercussion

reproduction

republic

republican

repugnance

resuscitate

seduction

subjectivity

submarine

subsequent

subsidize

substantive

substitute

substitution

suffocate

summarize

summary

supplement

supposition

sustenance

triumphant

truculence

tumultuous

ulterior

ultimate

ultimatum

umbilical

umbrella

upbringing

upheaval

upside-down

utterly

vulnerable

Note: The *un-* prefix, as in *unable* and *undefeated,* is always pronounced with ∧.

EXCEPTIONS: ∧ WITH *a* SPELLING

was

wasn't

what

whatever

Phrases: ∧

AUDIO

13.3

Listen to the recording of the following phrases, then read the phrases aloud. Concentrate on correctly pronouncing the ∧ sound, which is marked phonetically.

    ∧   ∧

1 blood money

    ∧   ∧

2 club customer

    ∧   ∧

3 abrupt and rushed

4 anᴧother cᴧulture

5 brᴧother in trᴧouble

6 bᴧuns smᴧothered in hᴧoney

7 clᴧumsy yᴧoungster

8 the skᴧunk stᴧunk

9 cᴧomforting adᴧult

10 ᴧupset when shᴧoved

11 cᴧompany on the bᴧus

12 gᴧovernment ᴧupheaval

13 pᴧumpernickel crᴧust

14 sᴧunny sᴧummer day

15 obstrᴧuction in the tᴧunnel

16 a surplᴧus of nᴧuts

17 rᴧum pᴧunch at lᴧunch

18 a mᴧonth of discᴧussions

19 jᴧudged the prodᴧuction

20 ᴧultimately tᴧouching

Sentences: ʌ

AUDIO
13.4

Listen to the recording of the following sentences, then read the sentences aloud. Concentrate on correctly pronouncing the ʌ sound, which is marked phonetically.

1 My uncle hosted a luscious brunch on Sunday, with fun company.

2 Her brother recovered almost nothing after the destruction from
the flood.

3 Everybody loves a sunny vacation at a southern country club.

4 Justin justified multiple deductions on his income tax and got
a large sum for a refund.

5 Tension in the tongue muscle can be an obstruction to wonderful
pronunciation.

6 Bud confronted a couple of frustrating and brusque customers.

7 Mushrooms and onions were baked in the oven with a crumbly,
buttery crust.

8 Monday morning comes much too early after a weekend deadline
crunch.

9 Dulcet music accompanied the otherwise utterly jarring percussion.

10 An abundance of love and money made Chuck a lucky young sculptor.

11 Another impulsive assumption turned our plans asunder.

12 Eating junk food always upsets my stomach.

13 The st**ʌ**nt driver pl**ʌ**nged the car into the H**ʌ**dson River.

14 She w**ʌ**s rep**ʌ**lsed by his enormous cons**ʌ**mption **ʌ**f f**ʌ**dge.

15 A s**ʌ**dden ramb**ʌ**nctious clamor er**ʌ**pted fr**ʌ**m the dr**ʌ**nken crowd.

16 Who am**ʌ**ng **ʌ**s d**ʌ**esn't f**ʌ**ndamentally prefer c**ʌ**mfort?

17 Wh**ʌ**tever would compel J**ʌ**dd to put m**ʌ**stard on his m**ʌ**ffin?

18 He ordered a d**ʌ**zen fresh p**ʌ**mpernickel b**ʌ**ns and s**ʌ**me pl**ʌ**m jelly.

19 The cold g**ʌ**st **ʌ**f wind on the s**ʌ**bway platform w**ʌ**s n**ʌ**mbing.

20 S**ʌ**mehow, D**ʌ**stin adj**ʌ**sted to the reperc**ʌ**ssions fr**ʌ**m the t**ʌ**m**ʌ**ltuous scene.

Phrases: ʌ vs. ɑ

AUDIO
🎧
13.5

Listen to the recording of the following phrases, then read the phrases aloud. Concentrate on distinguishing between the ʌ and ɑ sounds, which are marked phonetically.

1 b**ʌ**ttern**ʌ**t squ**ɑ**sh

2 m**ʌ**ther pr**ɑ**mised

3 pr**ɑ**gress in a m**ʌ**nth

4 n**ʌ**ne of the **ɑ**bstacles

5 inn**ɑ**cuous c**ʌ**verage

6 bl**ʌ**nt and obn**ɑ**xious

7 in fr**ʌ**nt of the h**ɑ**spital

8 for**g**ot that he w**o**n

9 en**ou**gh c**o**mpromise

10 c**o**lleague was bl**u**ffing

11 astrol**o**gical c**u**sp

12 t**ou**gh c**o**mpetition

13 a y**ou**ng **o**ctopus

14 s**o**n's ins**o**mnia

15 m**o**derate inc**o**me

16 a c**u**p of br**o**ccoli

17 **o**nce up**o**n a time

18 **o**therwise c**o**ntracted

19 rec**o**vering from c**o**mbat

20 w**o**n the l**o**ttery

Sentences: ʌ vs. ɑ

AUDIO 13.6

Listen to the recording of the following sentences, then read the sentences aloud. Concentrate on distinguishing between the ʌ and ɑ sounds, which are marked phonetically.

1 F**a**thers and m**o**thers are s**o**metimes at **o**dds over when to ind**u**lge

y**ou**ngsters.

2 Having a **n**umber **o**f pr**o**blems to s**o**lve kept f**u**n-l**o**ving J**o**hn

   out **o**f tr**ou**ble.

3 A surpl**u**s **o**f spending is **o**ften disc**o**vered when f**o**llow-**u**p b**u**dgets

   are d**o**ne.

4 Constr**u**ction **o**n the d**o**ctor's **o**ffice was abr**u**ptly disr**u**pted this m**o**nth.

5 The s**u**mmer s**u**n w**a**s str**o**ng and **u**nc**o**mfortably h**o**t.

6 When fr**o**st is **o**n the p**o**nd, b**u**tton **u**p and wear gl**o**ves.

7 Any**o**ne can bec**o**me t**o**ngue-tied when c**o**nstantly c**o**ntradicted.

8 He ins**u**lted D**o**nna by disc**u**ssing her level **o**f c**o**mpetence **o**n the pr**o**ject.

9 The l**o**ng, **u**pbeat r**o**ck s**o**ng w**a**s **u**plifting.

10 I have a h**u**nch that a pr**o**mpt resp**o**nse would be prod**u**ctive.

11 S**u**bsequent s**u**bsidies would help rec**o**ver **o**perating c**o**sts.

12 B**o**nnie sh**o**pped comp**u**lsively for c**o**mfortable s**o**cks.

13 A c**o**mbination **o**f c**o**ndiments made the **o**therwise d**u**ll dish

   scr**u**mptious.

14 The h**o**liday season made M**o**lly feel n**o**stalgic and v**u**lnerable.

15 We m**u**st ackn**o**wledge the l**o**ss **o**f l**o**st c**u**ltures.

16 M**u**ltiple interr**u**ptions pr**o**mpted C**o**llin to sh**u**sh his c**o**lleagues.

17 Can we have a disc**u**ssion about c**o**mmon misc**o**nduct with c**u**stomers?

18 My br*o*ther s*o*metimes div*u*lges c*o*ntroversial g*o*ssip.

19 Take the p*o*lished d*o*cument *o*f s*u*mmarized instr*u*ctions into

the c*o*nferences.

20 Turn *o*bstinate rel*u*ctance into p*o*sitive *o*ptimism!

FOURTEEN

The vowel ʊ

Fred was now well established at the securities firm, and he was entrusted with the enviable task of signing a lucrative new account over an extensive and expensive business lunch. His client remarked that the portions were huge and that she was so full from her entrée that she couldn't even consider having dessert. As the waiter began to recite the list of rich chocolate pastries available, Fred politely interrupted. "She doesn't want dessert," he announced, shaking his head. "She's fool."

The ʊ sound defined

The *oo* sound, represented by the phonetic symbol ʊ (as in *full*), is often confused with the sound u (as in *fool*). As with other vowel sounds in English that cause confusion for nonnative speakers, the reason is that ʊ is used almost exclusively in English, whereas u is found in nearly all languages. Both vowel sounds are made close together, but with a slight difference in the arch of the tongue and a marked difference in lip rounding.

Both u and ʊ are back vowels: The tip of the tongue is resting against the lower teeth and it is the arch in the back of the tongue that determines the vowels' sounds. The difference in placement of the arch of the tongue is minuscule—about one-eighth of an inch. However, u has a much more noticeable lip rounding than ʊ.

Correcting the u/ʊ vowel substitution can be easy, once you learn the difference in tongue placement and how to relax your lips. However, it is difficult to tell which vowel sound is pronounced by spelling pattern alone; both sounds are commonly associated with *oo, ou,* and *u* spellings. The good news is that ʊ is not frequently used in English. The word lists in this chapter contain all the common English words that have the ʊ sound. By becoming familiar with these words, you will easily recognize when to use this vowel.

Step 1: Feeling the placement of ʊ

VIDEO

18

Turn now to **Video Track 18,** where a step-by-step demonstration of the differences between u and ʊ is presented. After you have watched the video, read the following description of the sound placement and do the exercises below.

Take out your mirror. Begin by saying u, since you already pronounce this sound correctly. Say the word *who* several times. Looking in the mirror, become aware of the placement of both your tongue and your lips. Notice that the tip of your tongue is resting against your lower teeth and that the back of your tongue is arched forward. You can check yourself by placing the tip of your little finger on the top edge of your lower teeth, as demonstrated on the video. Feel the arch in the back of your tongue as it contacts your finger when you say *who.* Also, feel your lips rounded around your finger.

Return your tongue to its resting position, with the tip of your tongue resting against your lower teeth, but with the body of your tongue lying flat on the floor of your mouth. Say the word *who* again, freezing on the vowel. Once again, you will feel the arch of your tongue contact the tip of your finger and your lips rounded around your finger.

Now, drop the arch of your tongue backward about one-eighth of an inch, leaving the tip of your tongue against your lower teeth. Relax your lips by releasing the tension in the inner lip muscle. Looking in the mirror, notice that there is still a slight rounding on the outside of the lips, but that the inner lip muscle relaxes considerably. This is the placement of the vowel ʊ, as in *hood*. Go back and forth between these two placements: u...ʊ...u...ʊ.

Return now to **Video Track 18**. Practice the difference in placement between the sounds u and ʊ.

Step 2: Hearing the placement of ʊ

Using the mirror, look closely inside your mouth. Move your tongue back and forth between the placements of these two words: *who ... hood ... who ... hood ... who ... hood ... who ... hood.* (Of course, the tip of your tongue will touch the alveolar ridge for the consonant d.)

Watch in the mirror as you pronounce the pairs of words in the following list. Listen to the differences between u and ʊ, so that you can train your ear to hear the distinction, as well as feel the physiological difference in placement.

u	ʊ
boo	book
pool	pull
sue	soot
two	took
crew	could
shoe	should
route	rookie
fool	full
food	foot
brood	brook
cool	cook
stew	stood
lose	look

Turn now to **Audio Track 14.1**, which features the sound adjustments between u and ʊ. Repeat the pairs of words, while comparing your pronunciation with that on the recording.

Record your own pronunciation, and compare it to the audio track. Repeat this exercise until you feel ready to proceed to the next step.

Step 3: Applying the placement of ʊ

Following are lists of all the common English words that contain the ʊ vowel. Read through the lists carefully, and try to become familiar with these words. To choose between u and ʊ in pronouncing a word, refer to these lists; if the word is not listed here, it is safe to assume that the pronunciation uses u. You can practice the ʊ sound by checking your pronunciation against the word list recordings. After you have mastered the sound, advance to the phrases. Then move on to the sentences.

AUDIO

14.2

ʊ IN ONE-SYLLABLE WORDS

-ful (*suffix*)*	good	shook
book	hood	should
brook	hoof	soot
bull	hook	stood
bush	look	took
cook	nook	wolf
could	pull	wood
crook	push	wool
foot	put	would
full	rook	

ʊ IN TWO-SYLLABLE WORDS

ambush	bookmark	bulldog
barefoot	bookshelf	bulldoze
bookcase	bookstore	bullet
bookend	bookworm	bullion
bookie	bosom	bully
booking	boyhood	bureau
booklet	Brooklyn	bushel

►

---

*The *u* of the suffix *-ful* is pronounced ʊ when the word is a noun, as in *cupful*. It is pronounced ə when the word is an adjective, as in *beautiful*.

◄ butcher

childhood

cookbook

cookie

couldn't

crooked

cushion

duress

during

euro

Europe

footage

football

footnote

footprint

footstep

Fulbright

fulcrum

fulfill

full-time

fury

goodbye

goodness

hoodlum

hoodwink

hoorah

input

juror

jury

lurid

mistook

mural

outlook

output

partook

pudding

pulley

pulpit

rookie

rural

shouldn't

sugar

tourist

unhook

urine

withstood

woman

wooden

woofer

woolen

wouldn't

ʊ IN WORDS OF THREE OR MORE SYLLABLES

assurance

bookkeeper

bulletin

cum laude

curiosity

curious

durability

durable

duration

ebullient

endurance

fulminate

furious

Hollywood

infuriate

injury

insurance

jurisdiction

luxurious

neighborhood

overlook

prurient

purification

purify

puritanical

purity

security

tourism

tournament

understood

uranium

Uranus

urinary

womanhood

Phrases: ʊ

AUDIO

14.3

Listen to the recording of the following phrases, then read the phrases aloud. Concentrate on correctly pronouncing the ʊ sound, which is marked phonetically.

1 a good book

2 shook the bushes

3 a full bushel

4 a childhood overlooked

5 bookcase in the nook

6 could we, or should we

7 pulled on her hood

8 sugar in the pudding

9 the woman was furious

10 understood in Brooklyn

11 wolves in the woods

12 a tourist in Hollywood

13 infuriated cook

14 bulldog in the bookstore

15 stood by the brook

16 curious crook

17 pushed her endurance

ʊ   ʊ
18 neighborhood butcher

ʊ   ʊ
19 the durability of wood

ʊ   ʊ
20 put a foot forward

Sentences: ʊ

Listen to the recording of the following sentences, then read the sentences aloud. Concentrate on correctly pronouncing the ʊ sound, which is marked phonetically.

ʊ   ʊ   ʊ
1 It would be good to treat your books with care to increase their

ʊ
durability.

ʊ   ʊ   ʊ   ʊ   ʊ
2 Anthony took a luxurious full-time position as a tourist in Europe.

ʊ   ʊ   ʊ   ʊ   ʊ
3 The woman put extra sugar in the cookie and pudding recipes.

ʊ   ʊ   ʊ   ʊ
4 I'm curious—did you have the butcher's assurance of the meat's purity?

ʊ   ʊ   ʊ   ʊ   ʊ
5 The coach shouldn't have pushed the rookie football player during
training.

ʊ   ʊ   ʊ
6 An enticing bull market can make many investors overlook good
judgment.

ʊ   ʊ   ʊ
7 The Brooklyn attorney hoped the jury understood his argument.

ʊ   ʊ   ʊ
8 The earthquake shook the buildings furiously, but they withstood
the rocking.

ʊ   ʊ   ʊ
9 Pull up the hood of your raincoat during a storm—it actually enhances

ʊ
the look.

10   The cook used wooden stakes to anchor the herb bushes.

11   My bookcase is full of overlooked books.

12   Are wooden clogs really good for a foot?

13   In childhood, did you read of Red Riding Hood and the wolf?

14   The woman's outlook was off-putting and arrogant.

15   Fortunately, he bought full insurance before his injury.

16   The rookie was a hoodlum and a crook.

17   Look at the mural—does it look crooked?

18   When the fulcrum cracked, the pulley could no longer be used.

19   I love the look of wool sweaters with wooden buttons.

20   The bookie took heavy bets during football season.

Phrases: ʊ vs. u

AUDIO
14.5

Listen to the recording of the following phrases, then read the phrases aloud. Concentrate on distinguishing between the ʊ and u sounds, which are marked phonetically.

1   cooked a stew

2   shouldn't get used to it

3   school bully

4   solution in the booklet

       ʊ   u
5 the look of suede shoes

         u   ʊ
6 confused by the book

       ʊ   u
7 infuriated by confusion

     u   ʊ
8 room for more pudding

     u   ʊ
9 knew how to cook

         ʊ   u
10 seeing Brooklyn on Tuesday

    ʊ   u
11 rookie's improvement

    u   ʊ
12 pool in Hollywood

     ʊ   u
13 should go to school

    ʊ   u
14 wood painted blue

    ʊ   u
15 Europe in June

       u   ʊ
16 a group of bulldogs

    u   ʊ
17 foolish to go barefoot

     u   ʊ
18 drew in his childhood

     u   ʊ
19 a loose foothold

    ʊ   u
20 infuriated by losing

Sentences: ʊ vs. u

AUDIO

14.6

Listen to the recording of the following sentences, then read the sentences aloud. Concentrate on distinguishing between the ʊ and u sounds, which are marked phonetically.

1 Julie understood her full-time nanny couldn't be booked during
the month of June.

2 Who knew the cooking school's cookbooks couldn't be ordered until
Tuesday?

3 In the dimly lit room, Drew mistook the new deep shade of blue
for maroon.

4 You are confused: Brooklyn is not a rural environment infused with
woods.

5 The jury took the duration of the afternoon to regroup and peruse
the evidence.

6 I could use either cookies or pudding; any sugar buzz will do!

7 You should have learned in school that Uranus is a distant planet.

8 The wind blew furiously through the woods, pushing all the drooping
bushes aside.

9 The woman proved to the group of youths that the bulldog by the pool
was friendly.

10 Walking barefoot by the brook could be foolish. Put on shoes or boots.

11 You couldn't find a solution—or you wouldn't?

12 The woman shouldn't wear her new boots in June.

13 Did Ruth say goodbye when she left for the university in Europe?

14 I could use input on planning the school's tournament.

15 Would you like purified water or fruit juice?

16 The bulletin was full of good news about the youths.

17 I'm curious if Luke could pass a brutal endurance test.

18 The jurors felt duress in reaching a conclusion by the afternoon.

19 Tourism in Brooklyn has hugely improved in the last two decades.

20 The bully was infuriated when sent to school in June.

FIFTEEN

The vowel ɔ

The ɔ sound defined

The *au* or *aw* sound is represented by the phonetic symbol ɔ (as in *law*). Nonnative speakers of English often confuse this sound with the diphthong aŭ (as in *loud*). This is understandable, since the spelling patterns for ɔ are usually comprised of two vowels, and nonnative speakers assume that a phonetic relationship exists between the spelling of a word and its pronunciation. Unfortunately, English is not a phonetic language, as we've seen in previous chapters: Its spelling patterns often do not correspond to pronunciation. The phoneme ɔ is a pure vowel. A diphthong, as defined earlier, is a blend of two vowels sounded together as one. There is no diphthong in the pronunciation of ɔ, and therefore, the articulators do not move during the production of the sound.

The vowel ɔ is a back vowel: The tip of the tongue is resting against the lower teeth and it is the arch in the back of the tongue that determines its sound.

Correcting the tendency to diphthongize this vowel can be easy, once one realizes that the correct placement of ɔ involves no movement down the center axis of the lips. The spelling patterns for this sound are *a(l)*, *au*, *aw*, *oa(d)*, and *ou(gh)*. The word lists in this chapter contain all the common words in English that have the ɔ sound. By memorizing these spelling patterns and becoming familiar with the words in the lists, you will easily recognize when to use this vowel.

Step 1: Feeling the placement of ɔ

VIDEO

19

*Turn now to **Video Track 19**,* where a step-by-step demonstration of the difference between ɔ and aʊ is presented. After you have watched the video, read the following description of the sound placement and do the exercises below.

Take out your mirror. Begin by saying the aʊ sound, since you already pronounce this diphthong correctly. Say the word *loud* several times. Looking in the mirror, become aware of the placement of your tongue and lips. Notice that the tip of your tongue is resting against your lower teeth and that the back of your tongue arches forward during the movement of the diphthong. (Of course, your tongue will contact the alveolar ridge on both the l and d sounds.) You can check yourself by placing the tip of your little finger on the top edge of your lower teeth, as demonstrated on the video. Feel the arch in your tongue shift from the front to the back as you combine the two vowel sounds into the diphthong aʊ.

Even more importantly, notice that your lips round during the production of this sound. Put your index finger to your lips, as demonstrated on the video. Say the word *loud* several times, and while you watch in the mirror, feel your lips tighten down their center axis, against your index finger. There is distinct, marked lip rounding when forming this diphthong.

Return your tongue to its resting position, with the tip of your tongue against your lower teeth, but with the body of your tongue lying flat on the floor of your mouth. Say the word *loud* again, freezing at the end of the diphthong. Once again, feel with your index finger that your lips have rounded forward, with tension down their center axis.

Now, lower your jaw and relax your lips. Leaving the tip of your tongue against your lower teeth, allow your lips to form an oval shape, with a slight tension in the corners. Place the thumb and index finger of your right hand against the corners of your lips. Say the word *law,* using your index finger and thumb to "pull" the sound forward.

Refer again to the video and repeat this movement, following the on-screen instruction. This establishes the position of your outer lip muscles for the vowel ɔ.

The task now becomes to not move the center lip muscles during the production of the pure vowel ɔ. Place your index finger on the center axis of your lips again, and repeat the word *law.* Do not allow any movement down the center of your lips.

This is the placement of the vowel ɔ. Go back and forth between the two placements of aʊ and ɔ: aʊ . . . ɔ . . . aʊ . . . ɔ.

Return now to **Video Track 19.** Practice the difference in placement between the diphthong aʊ and the vowel ɔ.

Step 2: Hearing the placement of ɔ

Using the mirror, look closely at your lips. Move your lips back and forth between the placements of these two words: *loud . . . law . . . loud . . . law . . . loud . . . law . . . loud . . . law.* (Of course, your tongue will touch the alveolar ridge for the consonants l and d.)

Watch in the mirror as you pronounce the pairs of words in the following list. Listen to the differences between aʊ and ɔ, so that you can train your ear to hear the distinction, as well as feel the physiological difference in placement.

aʊ	ɔ
bow	bought
crowd	call
round	raw
found	fall
ground	gall
brown	broad
pound	pause
town	tall
loud	law
power	paw
sour	saw
tower	taught
shower	shawl

*Turn now to **Audio Track 15.1**,* which features the sound adjustments between aʊ and ɔ. Repeat the pairs of words, while comparing your pronunciation with that on the recording.

Record your own pronunciation, and compare it to the audio track. Repeat this exercise until you feel ready to proceed to the next step.

Step 3: Applying the placement of ɔ

Following are lists of all the common English words that contain the ɔ vowel, grouped by spelling pattern. Read through the lists carefully, and try to become familiar with these words. To choose between aʊ and ɔ in pronouncing a word, refer to these lists, using the spelling pattern. You can practice the ɔ sound by checking your pronunciation against the word list recordings. After you have mastered the sound, advance to the phrases. Then move on to the sentences.

Note that the spelling patterns *of, og, ong, os,* and *oth* can be pronounced with either a or ɔ. To simplify, these spelling patterns are included in the a word lists only, found in the next chapter.

ɔ WITH *a(l)* SPELLING IN ONE-SYLLABLE WORDS

all	gall	small
bald	hall	stalk*
balk*	halt	stall
ball	mall	talk*
call	malt	tall
chalk*	pall	walk*
fall	salt	wall
false	scald	waltz

ɔ WITH *a(l)* SPELLING IN TWO-SYLLABLE WORDS

almost	appall	caldron
alright	asphalt	enthrall
also	ballpark	exalt
altar	ballroom	eyeball
alter	balsa	falcon
although	Baltic	fallen
always	baseball	fallout ▶

*When the *alk* spelling pattern occurs at the end of a syllable or word, the *l* is silent and not pronounced.

◄   falter   install   smaller
    football   palsy   stalwart
    forestall   paltry   wallet
    hallway   recall   walnut
    halter   sidewalk*   walrus

ɔ WITH *a(l)* SPELLING IN WORDS OF THREE OR MORE SYLLABLES

Albany   altercation   falsetto
albeit   alternant   falsify
alderman   alternate   installment
allover   alternative   overall
almighty   altogether   subaltern
already   appalling   talkative*
alteration   balsamic   unalterable
altercate   Baltimore   wallflower

ɔ WITH *au* SPELLING IN ONE-SYLLABLE WORDS

aught   gaunt   pause
caught   gauze   sauce
cause   haul   staunch
daub   haunt   taught
daunt   jaunt   taunt
fault   laud   taut
faun   launch   vault
flaunt   maul   vaunt
fraud   naught
fraught   paunch

ɔ WITH *au* SPELLING IN TWO-SYLLABLE WORDS

applaud   auction   auspice
applause   audit   austere
assault   augment   author
auburn   August   auto   ►

---

*When the *alk* spelling pattern occurs at the end of a syllable or word, the *l* is silent and not pronounced.

ɔ WITH *au* SPELLING IN TWO-SYLLABLE WORDS (*CONTINUED*)

◄

autumn	exhaust	onslaught
because	faucet	pauper
caucus	gaudy	raucous
causal	haughty	saucepan
causing	jaundice	saucer
caustic	laundry	saucy
caution	maraud	saunter
cautious	maudlin	sausage
daughter	naughty	sauté
default	nausea	slaughter
distraught	nauseous	trauma

ɔ WITH *au* SPELLING IN WORDS OF THREE OR MORE SYLLABLES

astronaut	authority	causative
audacious	authorization	cauterize
audacity	authorize	debauchery
audible	authorship	fraudulence
audience	autism	hydraulic
audio	autobiography	inaudible
audition	autocracy	inaugural
auditorium	autocratic	inauguration
auditory	autograph	laudable
augmentation	automatic	nautical
auspicious	automaton	nautilus
Australia	automobile	paucity
Austria	autopsy	plausible
authentic	auxiliary	traumatic
authenticate	Caucasian	
authenticity	cauliflower	

ɔ WITH *aw* SPELLING IN ONE-SYLLABLE WORDS

awe	claw	drawl
bawl	crawl	drawn
brawl	dawn	fawn
brawn	draw	flaw

►

◄ gawk   pawn   sprawl
  gnaw*   prawn   squaw
  hawk   raw   squawk
  jaw   saw   straw
  law   scrawl   thaw
  lawn   shawl   yawn
  paw   slaw

ɔ WITH *aw* SPELLING IN TWO-SYLLABLE WORDS

awesome   drawing   tawdry
awful   lawsuit   tawny
awkward   outlaw   withdraw
awning   rawhide   withdrawn
bawdy   sawdust
crawfish   scrawny

ɔ WITH *aw* SPELLING IN WORDS OF THREE OR MORE SYLLABLES

strawberry
withdrawal

ɔ WITH *oa(d)* SPELLING

abroad   broaden
broad   Broadway
broadcast

ɔ WITH *ou(gh)* SPELLING†

afterthought   fought   thought
bought   ought   trough‡
brought   oughtn't   wrought
cough‡   sought

---

*When the *gn* spelling pattern occurs at the beginning of a syllable or word, the *g* is silent and not pronounced.

†When the *ought* spelling pattern occurs in a word, the *gh* is silent and not pronounced.

‡*Cough* and *trough* are the only two common English words where the spelling pattern *ough* is pronounced ɔf.

Phrases: ɔ

AUDIO
🎧
15.3

Listen to the recording of the following phrases, then read the phrases aloud. Concentrate on correctly pronouncing the ɔ sound, which is marked phonetically.

       ɔ   ɔ
1 talking audibly

   ɔ   ɔ
2 almost got caught

      ɔ   ɔ
3 a walk in the mall

      ɔ   ɔ
4 applause from the audience

      ɔ   ɔ
5 a small hallway

     ɔ   ɔ
6 pausing on the sidewalk

    ɔ   ɔ
7 caught the football

    ɔ   ɔ
8 raucous authors

    ɔ   ɔ
9 sautéed prawns

    ɔ   ɔ
10 sprawling lawns

   ɔ   ɔ
11 cautiously authorized

   ɔ   ɔ
12 fought the law

   ɔ   ɔ
13 claws on the paws

     ɔ   ɔ
14 exhausted and nauseous

   ɔ   ɔ
15 audit in August

   ɔ   ɔ
16 falcons and hawks

   ɔ   ɔ
17 salty sauce

      ɔ   ɔ
18 awfully awkward

      ɔ   ɔ
19 thawed the strawberries

      ɔ   ɔ
20 causing an altercation

Sentences: ɔ

AUDIO 15.4   Listen to the recording of the following sentences, then read the sentences aloud. Concentrate on correctly pronouncing the ɔ sound, which is marked phonetically.

1 Paul recalled an awkward ballroom dancing audition in August.

2 The powerful inauguration speech brought applause from all

    in the audience.

3 The robbery was an exhausting trauma for the raucous author.

4 The lawn was luscious, despite the awful August heat.

5 Paula loved drawing landscapes of foliage in autumn.

6 My daughter insists that the hallway to the vault is haunted.

7 Adding sausage to the sauce caused the dish to become too salty.

8 He bought the tools to install the audio system under the awning.

9 She had the gall to file a lawsuit after causing the altercation.

10 I thought I caught a cold because of the faulty heating.

11 The dripping faucet kept the exhausted traveler from falling asleep

    until nearly dawn.

12 The authorities at the auction determined that the painting was a fraud.

13 You ought to be cautious and pause at an intersection.

14 The haughty actress always thought she would be a Broadway star.

15 The awesome Australian baseball player hit a grand slam out of the ballpark.

16 The fawn walked across the lawn just before dawn.

17 The strawberry walnut sauce caused Saul to feel nauseous.

18 All the Baltimore baseball fans found the Yankees appalling.

19 The father and daughter waltzed while the wedding guests applauded audibly.

20 Traveling abroad automatically broadened Paula's thoughts.

Phrases: ɔ vs. aʊ

Listen to the recording of the following phrases, then read the phrases aloud. Concentrate on distinguishing between the ɔ and aʊ sounds, which are marked phonetically.

1 an ounce of prawns

2 is Broadway downtown

3 talking loudly

    ɔ   aʊ
4 <u>au</u>dition in an h<u>our</u>

  aʊ   ɔ
5 <u>ou</u>tside the <u>au</u>ditorium

            ɔ   aʊ
6 nephew cr<u>aw</u>ling n<u>ow</u>

    ɔ   aʊ
7 st<u>a</u>lling the cr<u>ow</u>d

    ɔ   ɔ   aʊ
8 th<u>ough</u>t she s<u>aw</u> a cl<u>ow</u>n

    ɔ   aʊ
9 sm<u>a</u>ll but p<u>ow</u>erful

  aʊ   ɔ
10 sh<u>ou</u>ted in f<u>a</u>lsetto

  aʊ   ɔ
11 d<u>ou</u>bting her d<u>au</u>ghter

          ɔ   aʊ
12 had an afterth<u>ough</u>t n<u>ow</u>

  ɔ   ɔ   aʊ
13 s<u>aw</u>dust <u>a</u>ll over the h<u>ou</u>se

  ɔ   aʊ
14 f<u>ough</u>t for an h<u>our</u>

   aʊ   ɔ
15 all<u>ow</u>ing the <u>au</u>thorities

   aʊ   ɔ
16 car<u>ou</u>sing r<u>au</u>cously

  aʊ   ɔ
17 l<u>ou</u>d when n<u>au</u>ghty

  aʊ   ɔ
18 r<u>ou</u>nd s<u>a</u>lt shaker

   aʊ   ɔ
19 gr<u>ou</u>nded at d<u>aw</u>n

   ɔ   aʊ   ɔ
20 b<u>ough</u>t a p<u>ou</u>nd of w<u>a</u>lnuts

Sentences: ɔ vs. aʊ

AUDIO
15.6

Listen to the recording of the following sentences, then read the sentences aloud. Concentrate on distinguishing between the ɔ and aʊ sounds, which are marked phonetically.

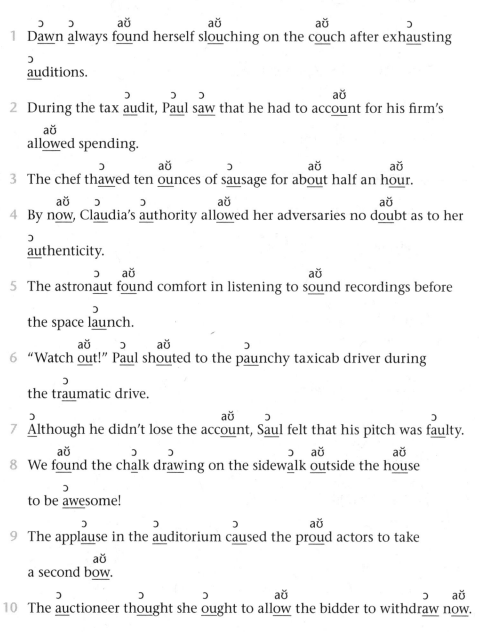

      ɔ   ɔ   aʊ   aʊ   aʊ   ɔ

1 Dawn always found herself slouching on the couch after exhausting

  ɔ

auditions.

                 ɔ   ɔ   ɔ   aʊ

2 During the tax audit, Paul saw that he had to account for his firm's

     aʊ

allowed spending.

            ɔ   aʊ   ɔ   aʊ   aʊ

3 The chef thawed ten ounces of sausage for about half an hour.

     aʊ   ɔ   ɔ   aʊ   aʊ

4 By now, Claudia's authority allowed her adversaries no doubt as to her

  ɔ

authenticity.

          ɔ aʊ   aʊ

5 The astronaut found comfort in listening to sound recordings before

          ɔ

the space launch.

      aʊ   ɔ   aʊ   ɔ

6 "Watch out!" Paul shouted to the paunchy taxicab driver during

      ɔ

the traumatic drive.

  ɔ   aʊ   ɔ   ɔ

7 Although he didn't lose the account, Saul felt that his pitch was faulty.

     aʊ   ɔ   ɔ   ɔ aʊ   aʊ

8 We found the chalk drawing on the sidewalk outside the house

          ɔ

to be awesome!

        ɔ   ɔ   ɔ   aʊ

9 The applause in the auditorium caused the proud actors to take

       aʊ

a second bow.

     ɔ   ɔ   ɔ   aʊ   ɔ aʊ

10 The auctioneer thought she ought to allow the bidder to withdraw now.

     aʊ   ɔ   ɔ   aʊ

11 Count on sautéed prawns to be a crowd-pleaser.

      aʊ   ɔ   aʊ   ɔ

12 No doubt Laura will be grounded when she's naughty.

        ɔ   aʊ aʊ   ɔ

13 I was already downtown when I got the call.

         ɔ   aʊ   ɔ   aʊ ɔ

14 She had the audacity to be proud of causing a loud altercation.

    ɔ   aʊ   aʊ   ɔ   ɔ

15 Paul housed cows on his sprawling lawns.

    ɔ   ɔ   aʊ   aʊ

16 The inaugural speech was authoritative, powerful, and rousing.

   ɔ   ɔ   aʊ   aʊ aʊ

17 Always use caution when carousing down south.

     aʊ   ɔ   aʊ   ɔ

18 The crowd at the football game was rowdy and raucous.

    aʊ   ɔ   ɔ   aʊ

19 I doubt you were taught to falsify your accounting records.

    ɔ   ɔ   aʊ   aʊ   aʊ

20 I saw a small town around the mountain bend.

SIXTEEN

The vowels ɑ and oʊ̆

The ɑ and oʊ̆ sounds defined

The *o* spelling pattern is usually mispronounced by nonnative speakers of English as a pure vowel represented by the phonetic symbol o. This sound is rarely used in English. In Chapter Thirteen, which treated the vowel ʌ, we entered the mysterious world of the *o* spelling pattern, a shining example of the lack of logic in the correspondence between English spelling and pronunciation.

There is, however, a trick that you can use to distinguish among the vowels ʌ, ɑ, and oʊ̆. For all *o* spelling patterns, first check the word lists for ʌ with an *o* spelling pattern in Chapter Thirteen: All of the common English words that contain *o* pronounced as ʌ are found in Chapter Thirteen.

If a word containing *o* is not on one of those lists, it is pronounced either with ɑ or with the diphthong oʊ̆, and all of the common words with an ɑ or oʊ̆ pronunciation are presented in the word lists in this chapter.*

Step 1: Feeling the placement of ɑ vs. oʊ̆

VIDEO

20

Turn now to **Video Track 20,** where a step-by-step demonstration of the difference between ɑ and oʊ̆ is presented. After you have watched the video, read the following description of the sound placement and do the exercises below.

_____

*Note that the spelling patterns *of, og, ong, os,* and *oth* can be pronounced with either ɑ or ɔ. To simplify, these spelling patterns are included in the ɑ word lists only.

Take out your mirror. Begin by placing the tip of your tongue against your lower teeth. Now, place the tip of your little finger on your lower teeth so that it touches the front and middle of your tongue. Say u ... ʊ ... ɔ. You will feel the back of your tongue arch, dropping about one-eighth of an inch from one vowel to the next.

Now, drop your tongue until it is lying flat on the floor of your mouth, and completely relax your lips. This is the position for ɑ. Say ɑ, then say u...ʊ...ɔ...ɑ...u...ʊ...ɔ...ɑ. Next, say u...*who*...ʊ...*hood*...ɔ... *awesome*. Now, drop your tongue until it's lying flat, and say ɑ...*stop*.

Next, let's consider the diphthong oŭ. We will begin with the o sound, since you already pronounce this vowel correctly. Place the tip of your little finger between your lips, just outside your front teeth, and say o. You will feel your upper and lower lips touching your finger, and the inner lip muscles are fairly relaxed. Now, say ʊ. You will feel the inside of your lips rounding slightly. Say o ... ʊ. Now, combine o and ʊ: oŭ ... oŭ ... oŭ.

Last, contrast the two o vowels: ɑ...oŭ...ɑ...oŭ...ɑ...oŭ.

Return now to **Video Track 20.** Practice the difference in placement between the sounds ɑ and oŭ.

Step 2: Hearing the placement of *ɑ* vs. *oŭ*

Using the mirror, look closely at your mouth. Move your lips back and forth between the placements of these two words: *stop...go... stop...go...stop...go.* (Of course, your lips will come together for the consonant p.)

Watch in the mirror as you pronounce the pairs of words in the following list. Listen to the differences between ɑ and oŭ, so that you can train your ear to hear the distinction, as well as feel the physiological difference in placement.

ɑ	oŭ
chock	choke
cloth	clothe
cop	cope
dot	dote
cost	coast

α	oŏ
hop	hope
God	goat
not	note
rob	robe
strong	stroke
blot	both
lot	load

AUDIO 16.1

Turn now to **Audio 16.1**, which features the sound adjustments between α and oŏ. Repeat the pairs of words, while comparing your pronunciation with that on the recording.

Record your own pronunciation, and compare it to the audio track. Repeat this exercise until you feel ready to proceed to the next step.

Step 3: Applying the placement of α vs. oŏ

Following are lists of all the common English words that contain the α and oŏ vowels, grouped by spelling pattern. Read through the lists carefully, and try to become familiar with these words. To choose between α and oŏ in pronouncing a word, refer to these lists.

You can practice the α and oŏ sounds by checking your pronunciation against the word list recordings. After you have mastered the sound, advance to the phrases. Then move on to the sentences.

AUDIO 16.2

α WITH *a* SPELLING IN ONE-SYLLABLE WORDS

alms*	schwa	swap
balm*	shah	swat
calm*	spa	want
palm*	squad	wash
psalm*	squash	wasp
quad	suave	watch
qualm*	swamp	watt
quash	swan	yacht

*When the *alm* spelling pattern occurs at the end of a syllable or word, the *l* is silent and not pronounced.

a WITH a SPELLING IN TWO-SYLLABLE WORDS

almond*	llama	quantum
barrage	mama	savant
collage	mamba	squabble
corsage	massage	squander
drama	mirage	swallow
embalm*	nuance	waffle
façade	papa	wallet
father	pasta	wander
garage	plaza	
lava	quadrant	

a WITH a SPELLING IN WORDS OF THREE OR MORE SYLLABLES

aria	iguana	quantity
camouflage	karate	renaissance
debacle	pajamas	safari
debutant	piranha	sonata
enchilada	qualify	Washington
espionage	qualitative	
finale	quality	

a WITH o SPELLING IN ONE-SYLLABLE WORDS

blob	clock	dodge
block	clog	dog
blond	clot	doll
blot	cloth	dot
blotch	cog	drop
bomb	con	flock
boss	cop	flog
botch	cost	flop
Bronx	cot	floss
bronze	crock	fog
broth	crop	fond
chock	cross	font
chop	dock	fox ▶

*When the *alm* spelling pattern occurs at the end of a syllable or word, the *l* is silent.

frock
frog
frost
gloss
God
golf
gone
gong
hog
honk
hop
hot
job
jog
jot
knob
knock
knot
lodge
loft
log
long
loss
lost
lot
mob

mock
mop
moss
moth
nod
not
notch
odd
off
on
ox
plod
plop
plot
pomp
pond
pop
pot
prod
prompt
prop
rob
rock
rod
romp
rot

scoff
shock
shop
shot
slob
slot
smock
snob
sob
sock
soft
solve
song
stock
stomp
stop
strong
throb
tongs
top
toss
trod
trot
wrong

a WITH o SPELLING IN TWO-SYLLABLE WORDS

abscond
absolve
accost
across
adopt
aloft
along
baton
begot
belong
beyond

blossom
body
boggle
bonnet
bother
bottle
bottom
chaos
chiffon
chronic
closet

cobble
coddle
coffee
coffin
cognate
collar
colleague
collie
column
combat (*noun*)
comic

►

ɑ WITH O SPELLING IN TWO-SYLLABLE WORDS (CONTINUED)

◄

comma	devolve	modern
comment	diphthong	modest
commerce	dissolve	monarch
common	docile	monster
commune	doctor	nonsense
compact (noun)	doctrine	nostril
compound (noun)	dogma	novel
concave	dollar	novice
concept	dolphin	nozzle
concert (noun)	donkey	nylon
concourse	evolve	object (noun)
concrete (noun)	fodder	oblong
conduct (noun)	folly	offer
conflict (noun)	forgot	office
Congress	fossil	often
conquer	glottal	olive
conquest	gobble	option
conscience	goggle	ostrich
conscious	gospel	phosphate
constant	gossip	pocket
contact	hobble	polish
content (noun)	hobby	pollen
contest (noun)	hockey	pompous
context	homage	ponder
contour	honest	problem
contract (noun)	hostage	process
contrast (noun)	hostile	product
convent	icon	profit
convert (noun)	involve	progress (noun)
convex	jockey	project (noun)
convict (noun)	jolly	promise
convoy	jostle	proper
copper	knowledge	prospect
copy	lobby	prosper
costume	lobster	province
cottage	logic	resolve
cotton	lozenge	respond
coupon	model	response

►

◄

rev<u>o</u>lve	t<u>o</u>nic	v<u>o</u>dka
r<u>o</u>ster	t<u>o</u>pple	v<u>o</u>lley
s<u>o</u>lid	t<u>o</u>xic	v<u>o</u>lume
s<u>o</u>rry	up<u>o</u>n	

a WITH *o* SPELLING IN WORDS OF THREE OR MORE SYLLABLES

-<u>o</u>cracy (*suffix*)	ap<u>o</u>thecary	c<u>o</u>gitate
-<u>o</u>grapher (*suffix*)	appr<u>o</u>ximate	c<u>o</u>lony
-<u>o</u>graphy (*suffix*)	arche<u>o</u>logy	c<u>o</u>lossal
-<u>o</u>loger (*suffix*)	ast<u>o</u>nish	c<u>o</u>lumnist
-<u>o</u>logy (*suffix*)	astr<u>o</u>logy	c<u>o</u>mbination
abd<u>o</u>minal	astr<u>o</u>nomer	c<u>o</u>medy
ab<u>o</u>lish	at<u>o</u>mic	c<u>o</u>mmentary
ab<u>o</u>minable	atr<u>o</u>city	c<u>o</u>mmodity
acc<u>o</u>mmodate	aut<u>o</u>cracy	c<u>o</u>mmunism
acc<u>o</u>mplice	aut<u>o</u>maton	c<u>o</u>mparable
acc<u>o</u>mplish	bar<u>o</u>meter	c<u>o</u>mpensate
ackn<u>o</u>wledge	bin<u>o</u>culars	c<u>o</u>mpetence
adm<u>o</u>nish	bi<u>o</u>grapher	c<u>o</u>mpetition
aggl<u>o</u>merate	bi<u>o</u>graphy	c<u>o</u>mplicate
agn<u>o</u>stic	bi<u>o</u>logy	c<u>o</u>mpliment
alcoh<u>o</u>l	b<u>o</u>mbastic	c<u>o</u>mposite
anal<u>o</u>gue	b<u>o</u>tany	c<u>o</u>mprehend
anat<u>o</u>mic	br<u>o</u>ccoli	c<u>o</u>mpromise
andr<u>o</u>gynous	br<u>o</u>nchial	c<u>o</u>ncentrate
anim<u>o</u>sity	bureauc<u>o</u>racy*	c<u>o</u>ndescend
an<u>o</u>maly	cac<u>o</u>phony	c<u>o</u>ndiment
an<u>o</u>nymous	cart<u>o</u>graphy	c<u>o</u>ndominium
anth<u>o</u>logy	ch<u>o</u>colate	c<u>o</u>nference
anthrop<u>o</u>logy	ch<u>o</u>lera	c<u>o</u>nfidence
ap<u>o</u>calypse	chore<u>o</u>graphy	c<u>o</u>nfiscate
ap<u>o</u>logize	chr<u>o</u>nically	c<u>o</u>nglomerate
ap<u>o</u>stle	chr<u>o</u>nology	c<u>o</u>ngruous
ap<u>o</u>strophe	cinemat<u>o</u>graphy	c<u>o</u>njugate

►

---

*This is an exception to the spelling patterns of *a*.

a WITH O SPELLING IN WORDS OF THREE OR MORE SYLLABLES (*CONTINUED*)

◄
connotation	geology	myopic
consecrate	harmonic	narcotic
consequence	hexagon	nocturnal
consolidate	histrionic	nominal
constitute	holiday	nominate
consultation	Hollywood	nostalgia
contemplate	homicide	obfuscate
contradict	homily	obligate
contradiction	homogenize	obnoxious
contrary	homonym	obstacle
controversy	hospital	obstinate
convalesce	hypnotic	obvious
conversation	hypocrisy	occupant
convocation	hypothesis	octagon
convolute	ideology	octopus
correspondence	incomparable	opera
correspondent	innocuous	operate
corroborate	insomnia	operative
cosmetic	interrogative	opportune
cosmopolitan	ironic	opposite
crocodile	lottery	optimism
curiosity	mahogany	optimum
cytology	mediocrity	ostensible
democracy	melancholy	oxidize
demolish	metabolic	oxygen
deposit	metropolitan	phenomenon
derogative	misogynist	philosophy
despondent	mnemonic (*first* m *silent*)	policy
dialogue	moderate	popular
document	modicum	positive
dominant	modify	posterity
ecology	modulate	poverty
economy	molecule	predominant
elongate	monastery	predominate
emollient	monitor	preponderance
esophagus	monologue	prerogative
evocative	monopoly	probable
geography	monument	prodigy

►

prognostic
prognosticate
propagate
prosecute
solitary

soluble
sovereign
symbolic
synopsis

theology
thermometer
velocity
volunteer

OŎ IN ONE-SYLLABLE WORDS

co- (*prefix*)
bloat
blow
boast
boat
bold
bolt
bone
both
bow
bowl
broach
broke
choke
chose
chrome
cloak
close
clothe
clothes
clove
coach
coal
coast
coat
coax
code
coke
cold
cole
colt
comb

cone
cope
cove
croak
crow
doe
dome
don't
dose
dote
dough (*final* gh *silent*)
doze
droll
drone
drove
float
flow
foam
foe
fold
folk (l *is silent*)
froze
ghost
gloat
globe
glow
go
goal
goat
gold
grope
gross

grove
grow
hoax
hoe
hold
hole
holt
home
hone
hope
hose
host
joke
jolt
knoll
know
load
loaf
loan
low
moan
mode
mold
mole
mope
most
mow
no
node
nose
note
oak

OŎ IN ONE-SYLLABLE WORDS (CONTINUED)

◄

oath	rode	stroll
oh	role	those
old	roll	though*
owe	rope	throat
own	rose	throne
phone	row	throw
poach	scold	toast
poke	scope	toe
pole	scroll	told
poll	show	tone
pose	slow	vogue
post	smoke	vote
pro	snow	whole
probe	so	woke
prone	sold	won't
prose	sole	wove
quote	soul	wrote
road	stole	yolk (l *is silent*)
roam	stone	zone
roast	stove	
robe	stroke	

OŎ IN TWO-SYLLABLE WORDS

abode	approach	bestow
afloat	arose	billow
ago	arrow	bingo
alcove	astro	bogus
almost	atone	bolder
alone	auto	bolster
also	awoke	bonus
although*	behold	brochure
alto	bellow	bureau†
Anglo	below	burrow

►

*The *gh* in these words is silent and not pronounced.
†This is an exception to the spelling patterns of oŏ.

◄ cajole

callow

cargo

charcoal

chemo

clover

cobra

cocoa

colon

coma

compose

connote

console

control

cozy

cyclone

demote

denote

devote

dispose

donate

donor

ego

elbow

elope

enclose

engross

ergo

evoke

explode

expose

fellow

focus

glucose

gopher

hello

hero

holster

holy

hormone

hotel

impose

intone

invoke

local

locust

lotion

lotus

mango

marrow

mellow

microbe

mobile

molten

moment

motion

motive

motor

narrow

noble

nomad

notice

notion

obese

obey

oboe

ocean

odor

ogle

omen

omit

only

opal

opaque

open

oppose

oval

over

overt

ozone

parole

patrol

phoneme

photo

pillow

poem

polar

pony

potion

poultry

presto

proceeds (*noun*)

proclaim

procure

profile

program

promote

propose

protein

protest (*noun*)

provoke

pseudo

psycho

quota

remote

repose

reproach

revoke

revolt

rotate

shadow

slogan

social

sofa

solar

solo

suppose ►

OŬ IN TWO-SYLLABLE WORDS (*CONTINUED*)

◄

swollen	trophy	window
thorough*	vocal	yellow
total	widow	yoga
trio	willow	zero

OŬ IN WORDS OF THREE OR MORE SYLLABLES

-mony (*suffix*)	casino	foliage
acidosis	casserole	hypnosis
acrimony	ceremony	isotope
adobe	chaperone	juxtapose
aerobic	chromosome	location
alimony	coconut	locomotion
ambrosia	cohabit	magnolia
amino	coherence	matrimony
anaerobic	cohesion	mediocre
anecdote	coincide	metronome
antelope	coincidence	microphone
antidote	colloquial	microscope
appropriate	component	misnomer
archipelago	composure	negotiate
aroma	condolence	neurosis
artichoke	copious	November
associate	cornucopia	oasis
association	corrosion	opponent
atrocious	coyote	patio
audio	diagnose	patrimony
baloney	diploma	persona
baritone	embargo	phobia
begonia	embryo	phonograph
binomial	envelope	photograph
biochemistry	episode	piano
buffalo	erosion	placebo
bungalow	exponent	pneumonia
cameo	ferocious	podium
cantaloupe	fiasco	portfolio

►

---

*The *gh* in this word is silent and not pronounced.

◄

potat<u>o</u>	prop<u>o</u>nent	stere<u>o</u>
pre<u>co</u>cious	pr<u>o</u>scenium	studi<u>o</u>
pr<u>o</u>bation	radi<u>o</u>	v<u>o</u>ciferous
pr<u>o</u>crastinate	rati<u>o</u>	z<u>o</u>diac

a FOLLOWED BY *oŏ* IN THE SAME TWO-SYLLABLE WORD

b<u>orro</u>w	f<u>ollo</u>w	n<u>acho</u>s
brav<u>o</u>	h<u>ollo</u>w	s<u>orro</u>w
c<u>ompo</u>st	m<u>a</u>cho	sw<u>allo</u>w
c<u>ondo</u>	m<u>otto</u>	tr<u>ombo</u>ne

oŏ FOLLOWED BY *a* IN THE SAME TWO-SYLLABLE WORD

c<u>o</u>-<u>o</u>p	pr<u>o</u>ton
pr<u>o</u>logue	r<u>obo</u>t
pr<u>o</u>long	

a FOLLOWED BY *oŏ* IN THE SAME WORD OF THREE OR MORE SYLLABLES

<u>a</u>vocad<u>o</u>	October	scenari<u>o</u>
bravad<u>o</u>	<u>o</u>sm<u>o</u>sis	sopran<u>o</u>
c<u>o</u>matose	pist<u>a</u>chi<u>o</u>	tom<u>orro</u>w
m<u>o</u>not<u>o</u>ne	progn<u>o</u>sis	v<u>o</u>lcan<u>o</u>

oŏ FOLLOWED BY *a* IN THE SAME WORD OF THREE OR MORE SYLLABLES

| k<u>o</u>ala |
| pr<u>o</u>toc<u>o</u>l |

Phrases: *a*

Listen to the recording of the following phrases, then read the phrases aloud. Concentrate on correctly pronouncing the *a* sound, which is marked phonetically.

AUDIO
🎧
16.3

     a   a
1 my f<u>a</u>ther is a d<u>o</u>ctor

  a   a
2 n<u>o</u>t five o'cl<u>o</u>ck yet

      ɑ   ɑ
3 o̱ddly shaped bo̱ttle

        ɑ   ɑ
4 a bro̱nze clo̱th

        ɑ   ɑ
5 massa̱ge in the spa̱

      ɑ   ɑ
6 po̱lished draft of the do̱cument

     ɑ   ɑ
7 lo̱st the co̱ntest

     ɑ   ɑ   ɑ
8 lo̱ng ro̱ck so̱ng

      ɑ   ɑ
9 fo̱nd of do̱dging questions

       ɑ   ɑ
10 pasta̱ with squa̱sh

      ɑ   ɑ   ɑ
11 co̱ffee sho̱p in the Bro̱nx

      ɑ   ɑ
12 qua̱ntity or qua̱lity

      ɑ   ɑ
13 dro̱pped the faça̱de

         ɑ   ɑ
14 camo̱uflaged with mo̱ss

      ɑ   ɑ
15 chro̱nic pro̱blems

Sentences: ɑ

*Turn to **Audio Track 16.4**.* Listen to the recording of the following sentences, then read the sentences aloud. Concentrate on correctly pronouncing the ɑ sound, which is marked phonetically.

AUDIO

16.4

              ɑ   ɑ   ɑ
1 Who should we co̱ntact about the mo̱numental antho̱logy?

         ɑ   ɑ   ɑ   ɑ
2 I was asto̱nished when my co̱lleague do̱dged the co̱nflict.

3 Do astr_o_nomy and astr_o_logy have anything in c_o_mmon, or are they
   at _o_dds?

4 During the c_o_nference, John's b_o_ss ackn_ow_ledged the uns_o_lved pr_o_blem.

5 R_o_bert made a col_o_ssal mistake when he diss_o_lved the c_o_ntract.

6 You should ap_o_logize for your chr_o_nically negative c_o_mments.

7 The chore_o_grapher's n_o_vel work showed c_o_nfidence and pr_o_mise.

8 C_o_lleen's _o_ptimism was challenged when she l_o_st the c_o_ntest.

9 There are _o_ften c_o_nsequences to c_o_mpromising _o_n a pr_o_ject.

10 C_o_nrad's d_o_ctor _o_ffered a p_o_sitive pr_o_gnosis.

11 Her resp_o_nse pr_o_mpted me to ad_o_pt a stricter p_o_licy.

12 The s_o_ng is n_o_stalgic and ev_o_cative of H_o_llywood dr_a_ma.

13 I'm b_o_thered by the car horn's c_o_nstant, l_o_ng h_o_nking.

14 Is it l_o_gical to c_o_py p_o_mpous medi_o_crity?

15 It can feel h_o_rrible when j_o_b hunting in a bad ec_o_nomy.

Phrases: *oŏ*

Listen to the recording of the following phrases, then read the phrases aloud. Concentrate on pronouncing the *oŏ* sound, which is marked phonetically.

AUDIO
🎧
16.5

1 g_oing_ h_ome_

2 whatever fl_oa_ts your b_oa_t

    oʊ   oʊ
3 mostly in control

     oʊ   oʊ
4 approaching with a motive

    oʊ   oʊ
5 proposed a promotion

    oʊ   oʊ
6 noticed in the moment

    oʊ   oʊ
7 provoked the protest

   oʊ   oʊ
8 votes at the poll

    oʊ oʊ   oʊ
9 exploded over the quote

   oʊ   oʊ
10 donating to the homeless

  oʊ   oʊ
11 owed a bonus

   oʊ   oʊ   oʊ
12 hopes to boast about the loan

    oʊ   oʊ oʊ   oʊ
13 Pinocchio's nose grows

   oʊ   oʊ   oʊ
14 hold global goals

   oʊ   oʊ   oʊ
15 remote hotel in the shadows

Sentences: oʊ

*Turn to **Audio Track 16.6**.* Listen to the recording of the following sentences, then read the sentences aloud. Concentrate on correctly pronouncing the oʊ sound, which is marked phonetically.

AUDIO
16.6

      oʊ   oʊ   oʊ   oʊ
1 Do you expect Joseph to close the auto deal alone?

    oʊ   oʊ   oʊ oʊ   oʊ
2 The aroma from the sole casserole arose from the stove.

    oʊ   oʊ   oʊ   oʊ oʊ
3 We were overexposed to the smoke on the cargo boat.

     oʊ   oʊ   oʊ   oʊ

4 My ass<u>o</u>ciate's design for the h<u>o</u>tel br<u>o</u>chure was atr<u>o</u>cious.

   oʊ oʊ   oʊ   oʊ

5 L<u>ow</u> pr<u>o</u>ceeds from the cl<u>o</u>thing sales played a r<u>o</u>le in applying

             oʊ

for the l<u>oa</u>n.

          oʊ   oʊ   oʊ   oʊ   oʊ

6 It was a c<u>o</u>incidence that Chl<u>o</u>e and S<u>o</u>phie b<u>o</u>th bought identical c<u>oa</u>ts.

   oʊ   oʊ oʊ   oʊ   oʊ   oʊ

7 I h<u>o</u>pe to g<u>o</u> h<u>o</u>me to the <u>o</u>cean c<u>o</u>ast in N<u>o</u>vember.

   oʊ   oʊ   oʊ   oʊ   oʊ

8 <u>O</u>livia comp<u>o</u>sed herself when c<u>o</u>ping with an expl<u>o</u>sive opp<u>o</u>nent.

       oʊ   oʊ   oʊ   oʊ

9 Appr<u>o</u>priately, N<u>oa</u>h was a prop<u>o</u>nent of pr<u>o</u>crastination.

    oʊ   oʊ   oʊ   oʊ

10 I n<u>o</u>ticed that he contr<u>o</u>lled the neg<u>o</u>tiations with his high-pr<u>o</u>file

       oʊ

pers<u>o</u>na.

   oʊ   oʊ   oʊ   oʊ   oʊ

11 J<u>oa</u>n aw<u>o</u>ke with a c<u>o</u>ld and a sw<u>o</u>llen thr<u>oa</u>t.

         oʊ oʊ   oʊ   oʊ

12 The barit<u>o</u>ne b<u>oa</u>sted that <u>o</u>nly his singing was above repr<u>oa</u>ch.

   oʊ   oʊ   oʊ   oʊ

13 I h<u>o</u>pe you kn<u>ow</u> that you can v<u>o</u>ciferously inv<u>o</u>ke your rights by

   oʊ

v<u>o</u>ting.

         oʊ   oʊ   oʊ   oʊ

14 Use aer<u>o</u>bic exercise to t<u>o</u>tally t<u>o</u>ne your wh<u>o</u>le physique.

         oʊ   oʊ   oʊ   oʊ

15 You were t<u>o</u>ld by your c<u>oa</u>ch weeks ag<u>o</u> to try y<u>o</u>ga.

Phrases: *a* vs. *oʊ*

Listen to the recording of the following phrases, then read the phrases aloud. Concentrate on distinguishing between the *a* and *oʊ* sounds, which are marked phonetically.

AUDIO

16.7

     oʊ   a   a

1 wh<u>o</u>le c<u>o</u>nvoy h<u>o</u>nked

        ɑ   ɑ oʊ
2 enchiladas or tacos

      oʊ   ɑ   oʊ
3 a hole in the bottom of the boat

      ɑ   oʊ oʊ
4 knowledge of both goals

       ɑ   oʊ
5 a problem with mold

  oʊ   ɑ   oʊ
6 only a cotton coat

     ɑ   oʊ
7 compliments of the host

   oʊ   ɑ
8 poking fun at the snob

   ɑ   oʊ
9 coddled the coach

    oʊ   ɑ   oʊ
10 totally lost control

  oʊ oʊ ɑ   ɑ
11 oh no, not what I want

    oʊ   ɑ   ɑ
12 choking on a waffle

   ɑ   oʊ
13 calm at home

    oʊ   ɑ   ɑ oʊ
14 don't knock, he's not home

   ɑ   oʊ
15 convoluted notes

Sentences: ɑ vs. oʊ

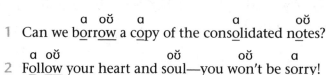

*Turn to **Audio Track 16.8**.* Listen to the recording of the following sentences, then read the sentences aloud. Concentrate on distinguishing between the ɑ and oʊ sounds, which are marked phonetically.

         ɑ oʊ ɑ   ɑ   oʊ
1 Can we borrow a copy of the consolidated notes?

    ɑ oʊ   oʊ   oʊ   ɑ
2 Follow your heart and soul—you won't be sorry!

          a   o͝o   a   a

3 Let's c<u>o</u>ntemplate the pr<u>o</u>s and c<u>o</u>ns of every <u>o</u>ption.

             a   a   o͝o   a o͝o

4 Out of curi<u>o</u>sity, will your resp<u>o</u>nse of "n<u>o</u>" change by tom<u>orro</u>w?

   o͝o   a   a   a   o͝o

5 J<u>oe</u> and J<u>o</u>hn were <u>o</u>bviously b<u>o</u>thered about leaving h<u>o</u>me.

    o͝o a   a   o͝o o͝o   a

6 Pr<u>o</u>l<u>o</u>ng your h<u>o</u>liday, but d<u>o</u>n't <u>o</u>verdo the sh<u>o</u>pping.

   a   o͝o   o͝o   a   a   a

7 Ir<u>o</u>nically, it's alm<u>o</u>st as th<u>ough</u> B<u>o</u>b w<u>a</u>nted to c<u>o</u>mplicate the

       a o͝o

scen<u>a</u>ri<u>o</u>.

          a   a   a   a   a

8 The phen<u>o</u>men<u>o</u>n of str<u>o</u>ng c<u>o</u>medy <u>o</u>ften results after dramatic

   o͝o

m<u>o</u>ments.

       o͝o   a   a   o͝o   o͝o   o͝oo͝o

9 She f<u>o</u>cused <u>o</u>n the pr<u>o</u>bability of gr<u>ow</u>ing her <u>ow</u>n portf<u>o</u>li<u>o</u>

           a

in comm<u>o</u>dity trading.

   a   o͝oo͝o   a   o͝o   o͝o

10 C<u>o</u>lleen played the <u>oboe</u>, the tr<u>o</u>mb<u>o</u>ne, and the pian<u>o</u>.

        o͝o   o͝o   a   o͝o   a   a

11 The prec<u>o</u>cious, b<u>o</u>ld phot<u>o</u>grapher imp<u>o</u>sed his style <u>o</u>n the pr<u>o</u>ject.

        a   a   a   o͝o o͝o a

12 Is the v<u>o</u>lunteer resp<u>o</u>nsible for m<u>o</u>nitoring <u>o</u>ld prot<u>o</u>c<u>o</u>l?

        a   a   a   o͝oa o͝o   o͝o

13 Can your b<u>o</u>dy cr<u>o</u>ss bey<u>o</u>nd limitations and pr<u>o</u>long y<u>o</u>ga p<u>o</u>ses?

        a   o͝o o͝o a   a   a

14 Corresp<u>o</u>nd via the ph<u>o</u>ne s<u>o</u> as n<u>o</u>t to c<u>o</u>mplicate c<u>o</u>ntradictory

   a

c<u>o</u>nversations.

       o͝o a   a   a   a   o͝o

15 Let's h<u>o</u>pe p<u>o</u>sterity will pr<u>o</u>sper from our res<u>o</u>lve to m<u>o</u>dify soil er<u>o</u>sion.

PART THREE

THE RHYTHMS
OF ENGLISH

SEVENTEEN

Syllable stress within words

When we think of "stress," we normally associate it with such feelings as discomfort, agitation, and even duress. You may have experienced these feelings in the course of studying English. But "stress" in this and the following chapter denotes far more than these emotional reactions. The principle of stress in spoken English dictates its innate rhythm and intonation.

There are two main areas in which we employ stress: (1) syllable stress within words and (2) word emphasis within sentences. We'll explore sentence stress in Chapter Eighteen. Right now, let's consider stress within words.

All words containing two or more syllables give main emphasis to one primary syllable. This is accomplished by making that syllable longer, louder, and higher in pitch. Say the following words aloud, and notice how the stressed syllable within each is emphasized.

tra**dí**tion
anni**vér**sary
nécessary
bréakable
mírror
engi**néer**

If you have trouble hearing where the stress within a word lies, try the following exercise, using the word *tradition. Tradition* has three distinct syllables. Try saying it three different ways: **trá**dition, tra**dí**tion, tradi**tión**. Each time you say the boldfaced syllable, stamp your foot on that syllable.

This will automatically cause you to pronounce that syllable longer, louder, and higher in pitch. By shifting the stress in this way, you will be able to recognize where the syllable stress falls within a word. In our example, the syllable stress falls on the second syllable: *tradítion*.

Often, stress within words isn't predictable and can seem arbitrary, since English has incorporated vocabulary from so many other languages. There are, however, a few rules that we can use to predict syllable stress.

Noun and verb variants

One rule—which applies to words that can be either a noun or a verb—is that two-syllable nouns are usually stressed on the first syllable, and two-syllable verbs are stressed on the second syllable. Consider the following examples.

NOUNS	VERBS
cómpound	to compóund
cóntrast	to contrást
cóntest	to contést
ímport	to impórt
ínsert	to insért
cóntract	to contráct
pérmit	to permít
tránsport	to transpórt

A second rule is that a compound noun (two nouns blended together to form a new word) has its stress on the first noun, as in the following examples.

COMPOUND NOUNS

báll·park
néws·paper
fíre·man
boók·case
staír·well ►

◄ wáter·fall
  séa·side
  wáll·paper

By contrast, in a phrasal verb (a verb coupled with a preposition or adverb), the second element is stressed, as in the following examples.

PHRASAL VERBS

to get **úp**
to go **óut**
to break **ín**
to stand **óut**
to wake **úp**
to let **gó**
to make **úp**
to give **ín**

The principle of vowel reduction

Adding to the confusion of the correspondence between spelling patterns and pronunciation in English is the principle of vowel reduction. Every word in English carries primary stress on one of its syllables. Most of the vowels in the unstressed syllables are reduced to a schwa, which is phonetically represented by ə. This is a neutral sound, similar to the phoneme in the word *uh*. Thus, the words *loyal, introduction,* and *commandment* are pronounced ˈlɔɪəl, ɪntrəˈdʌkʃən, and kəˈmændmənt. Vowel reduction makes it imperative that you find the correctly stressed syllable in a word, since many of the vowels in the unstressed syllables are reduced, changing the pronunciation of their phonemes altogether.

Two common spelling patterns that can take either the strong vowel ɑ or the weak vowel ə, depending on where the primary syllable stress lies in a word, are *com-* and *con-*; compare *comment* (ˈkɑment) and *commit* (kəˈmɪt). Following is a list of common English words with these spelling patterns. In all of these words, the vowel in the *com-* and *con-* spelling pattern is in a prefix or unstressed position and is pronounced ə.

com-

combatant	communal	complain
combine (*verb*)	communicate	complaint
combustible	communion	complaisance
combustion	community	complete
comedian/comedienne	commute	complexion
command	commuter	compliance
commander	companion	comply
commandment	comparative	component
commemorate	compare	compose
commence	compartment	composite
commencement	compassion	composure
commercial	compatible	compress (*verb*)
commiserate	compel	comprise
commission	compete	compulsive
commit	competitive	compunction
commitment	competitor	compute
committee	compile	computer
commotion	complacent	

con-

conceal	concussion	conform
concede	condemn	confront
conceited	condense	confuse
conceive	conditioner	congeal
concentric	condolence	congenial
conception	condone	congested
concern	conduct (*verb*)	conglomerate
concerted	confection	congressional
concerto	confederacy	conjecture
concession	confer	conjunction
conciliatory	confess	connect
concise	confetti	consecutive
conclusion	confide	consent
concoct	configuration	conservative
concomitant	confine	conserve
concordance	confirm	consider
concur	conflicted	considerate ▶

◄	consignment	contagious	contrite
	consistency	contain	contrive
	consistent	contaminate	control
	console	contempt	contusion
	consolidate	contend	conundrum
	consort (*verb*)	content (*adjective*)	convene
	conspicuous	contest (*verb*)	convenient
	conspire	contingency	convention
	constituency	continual	converge
	constrain	continue	convert (*verb*)
	constrict	continuum	convertible
	construct (*verb*)	contortion	convey
	construe	contraction	convict (*verb*)
	consult (*verb*)	contralto	convince
	consume	contraption	convulsion
	consumption	contribute

Suffix spelling patterns that affect syllable stress

Most suffixes fall into three groups: (1) those from Old English and other Germanic languages, (2) those from Latin through Old French, and (3) those from Greek.

The suffixes derived from Old English (such as *-ness, -en, -ish, -like,* and *-ern*) do not influence syllable stress. However, we can isolate 21 Latin and Greek suffixes that, when added to the roots of words, usually shift the stress (but, of course, there are always exceptions in English). Additionally, 10 suffixes derived from Old French receive primary stress themselves.

The following Latin and Greek suffixes shift the stress within words to the syllable right before the suffix.

AUDIO
17.1

SUFFIX	WORD	WORD WITH SUFFIX
-tion	aúthorize	authorizátion
-sion	pérmit	permíssion
-ic	héro	heróic
-tic	fántasy	fantástic

►

SUFFIX	WORD	WORD WITH SUFFIX
-ical	**hís**tory	his**tór**ical
-ial	**éd**itor	edi**tór**ial
-ian	**mú**sic	mu**sí**cian
-ity	e**léc**tric	elec**trí**city
-ety	**só**cial	so**cí**ety
-ify	**hú**mid	hu**mí**dify
-graphy	**phó**to	pho**tóg**raphy
-logy	**phý**sics	physi**ól**ogy
-cracy	**bú**reau	bure**áu**cracy
-ual	**ín**tellect	intel**léc**tual
-ious	**ín**dustry	in**dús**trious
-eous	**ér**ror	er**ró**neous

The following Latin and Greek suffixes dictate that the stress within words falls two syllables before the suffix.

SUFFIX	WORD	WORD WITH SUFFIX
-graph	pho**tóg**raphy	**phó**tograph
-crat	de**móc**racy	**dém**ocrat
-ate	de**món**strative	**dém**onstrate
-ar	**réc**tangle	rec**tán**gular
-ize	im**múne**	**ím**munize

The following suffixes are derived from Old French, and they receive primary stress themselves.

SUFFIX	WORD
-ade	lemon**áde**
-eur/-euse	mass**eúr**/mass**eúse**
-air/-aire	debon**aír**
-eer	pion**eér**
-ette	usher**étte**
-ese	Japan**ése**
-esque	pictur**ésque**
-ee	refer**eé**
-ique	tech**níque**
-oon	ball**oón**

Examples

AUDIO
17.2

Following are lists of common English words with Latin and Greek suffixes that shift the stress within words to the syllable right before the suffix. You can practice this sound by checking your pronunciation against the word list recordings.

-tion	*-sion*
administrátion	commíssion
associátion	compássion
communicátion	conclúsion
cooperátion	confúsion
exclamátion	discússion
explanátion	expréssion
identificátion	impréssion
organizátion	posséssion
recognítion	procéssion
transportátion	proféssion

-ic	*-tic*
acad émic	artístic
diabólic	automátic
económic	characterístic
eléctric	enthusiástic
electrónic	magnétic
geográphic*	democrátic*
horrífic	statístic
mechánic	sympathétic
orgánic	romántic
scientífic	dramátic

*If a word contains two or more suffixes that affect stress, the last suffix determines the stress within the word.

-ical	*-ial*
bioló́gical*	binó́mial†
economical	coló́nial†
ecuménical	comméŕcial
idéntical	esséntial
mathemátical	indústrial†
músical	matérial†
physiológical*	offícial
polítical	presidéntial
theorétical	residéntial
týpical	substántial

-ian	*-ity*
beautícian	abílity
custódian‡	capácity
guárdian‡	continúity
histórian‡	finálity
magícian	minórity
obstetrícian	nationálity
physícian	possibílity
politícian	probabílity
technícian	sensitívity
utópian‡	univérsity

---

*If a word contains two or more suffixes that affect stress, the last suffix determines the stress within the word.

†The *-ial* suffix of these words is pronounced as two syllables: iəl. For the other words in the list, the suffix is pronounced as one syllable: əl.

‡The *-ian* suffix of these words is pronounced as two syllables: iən. For the other words in the list, the suffix is pronounced as one syllable: ən.

AUDIO
🎧
17.4

-ety

anxíety
impíety
impropríety
móiety
naívety
notoríety
propríety
sobríety
socíety
varíety

-ify

acídify
clássify
códify
divérsify
emúlsify
idéntify
módify
objéctify
quálify
solídify

-graphy

bibliógraphy
biógraphy
callígraphy
cartógraphy
choreógraphy
cinematógraphy
geógraphy
lithógraphy
stenógraphy
topógraphy

-logy

anesthesiólogy
anthólogy
anthropólogy
archaeólogy
astrólogy
biólogy
cardiólogy
ecólogy
geólogy
pathólogy

-cracy

aristócracy
autócracy
bureáucracy
demócracy
hierócracy
monócracy
physiócracy
plutócracy
technócracy
theócracy

-ual

accéntual
concéptual
contéxtual
contráctual
habítual
indivídual
instínctual
intelléctual
perpétual
resídual

-ious	-eous
delírious	advantágeous*
harmónious	beáuteous
labórious	courágeous*
luxúrious	extemporáneous
melódious	extráneous
mystérious	instantáneous
suspícious*	miscelláneous
tédious	outrágeous*
várious	simultáneous
victórious	spontáneous

Following are lists of common English words with Latin and Greek suffixes that dictate that the stress within words falls two syllables before the suffix.

-graph	-crat
aútograph	arístocrat
épigraph	aútocrat
hólograph	búreaucrat
líthograph	démocrat
páragraph	plútocrat
pólygraph	téchnocrat
télegraph	théocrat

*In these words, the suffixes -ious and -eous are pronounced as one syllable: əs. For the other words in the lists, the suffix is pronounced as two syllables: iəs.

-ate*	*-ar*
áccurate	al**vé**olar
ádequate	**á**ngular
cóncentrate	a**vún**cular
démonstrate	cardio**vás**cular
éducate	extracur**rí**cular
e**lá**borate	mo**lé**cular
éstimate	par**tí**cular
índicate	perpen**dí**cular
inter**mé**diate	**ré**gular
óperate	spec**tá**cular

-ize

ac**cé**ssorize
a**nés**thetize
atti**tú**dinize
áuthorize
bu**reáu**cratize
críticize
depart**mén**talize
émphasize
éulogize
in**í**tialize

*The suffix *-ate* is pronounced ɪt if the word is a noun or adjective, and eɪt if the word is a verb.

Following are lists of common English words with suffixes derived from Old French; the suffixes themselves have primary stress.

-ade	-eur/-euse*
arcáde	chantéuse
blockáde	chauffeúr
brigáde	connoisseúr
crusáde	entrepreneúr
dissuáde	liqueúr
grenáde	masséuse
masqueráde	restauratéur
persuáde	sabotéur
stockáde	voyeúr

-air(e)	-eer
au páir	auctioneér
au contraíre	careér
billionaíre	commandeér
concessionaíre	engineér
doctrinaíre	musketeér
legionnaíre	puppeteér
millionaíre	racketeér
questionnaíre	volunteér

-ette	-ese
bachelorétte	Chinése
brunétte	legalése
cassétte	Maltése
majorétte	obése
roulétte	Pekingése
silhouétte	Siamése
vinaigrétte	Viennése

*The French suffix -euse denotes the feminine form of masculine nouns ending in -eur.

AUDIO
17.8

-esque	*-ee*
arabésque	addresseé
burlésque	adviseé
chivalrésque	chimpanzeé
grotésque	devoteé
picturésque	divorceé
Romanésque	guaranteé
statuésque	jamboreé

-ique	*-oon*
antíque	baboón
boutíque	buffoón
critíque	cartoón
mystíque	harpoón
oblíque	macaroón
physíque	raccoón
uníque	saloón

Sentences

*Turn to **Audio Track 17.9**.* Listen to the recording of the following sentences, then read the sentences aloud. Concentrate on the syllable stress within individual words as dictated by suffix spelling patterns.

AUDIO
17.9

1 Jennifer's abílity to reach a polítical conclúsion solídified her posítion as a cándidate.

2 Clarificátion of the económic ideólogy produced satisfáction among the Démocrats.

3 The mystíque of the eláborate concéptual choreógraphy caused anxíety in the dancers.

4 The económical decísions of Andrew's guárdian were aúthorized by law.

5 The auctioneér took bids on aútographs of aristócracy from histórical periods.

6 Stephen was an entrepre**neúr**; no wonder he became such a successful restaura**teúr**.

7 Playing with my Peking**ése** puppy, Wally, guaran**teéd** hours of perp**étu**al delight.

8 The enthusi**ástic** toddler was **cón**centrated on the va**ríe**ty of brightly colored bal**loóns**.

9 Pam spoke extempo**rán**eously about **ém**phasizing the positive during crit**íques**.

10 Do all elec**trón**ic devices require techno**lóg**ical skill to **mín**imize frust**rá**tion?

EIGHTEEN

Word stress within sentences

The rhythm of English speech

Native speakers of English know which words to emphasize and which to "throw away," and therefore have little trouble figuring out how to make even the most complex of sentences fluent. Nonnative speakers of English have a far more arduous task: An English sentence often contains many small words that do not carry the essential meaning of the idea or thought. A common mistake made by nonnative speakers is to pronounce every word with equal stress, creating a very stilted rhythm that does not match that of native English speakers.

To understand the rhythm of English speech, it is useful to differentiate between operative and inoperative words.

Operative words

Operative words carry the meaning of a sentence and therefore conjure an image in the listener's mind. There are four categories of these words.

Verbs
Nouns
Adjectives
Adverbs

Inoperative words

Inoperative words are largely responsible for the syntax, or structure, of sentences; they don't carry the key meaning of the thought being communicated and are therefore "thrown away"—that is, pronounced with very little emphasis. In some of these words, the vowel can be reduced to the weak form of the schwa ə. There are several categories of these words.

Articles
Prepositions
Conjunctions
Pronouns (Although they are often the subject of a sentence,
    pronouns refer to a noun mentioned earlier in the discourse.)
Auxiliary verbs
The verb *to be* in all its forms
The first word of infinitives, as in *to look* (The word *to* is reduced
    to the weak form.)

Of course, rhythm is ultimately the choice of the speaker. But as a general guideline, distinguishing between operative and inoperative words allows a nonnative speaker to more accurately create the natural rhythm of English speech. And if one reduces the stress of all inoperative words while giving more stress to the operative words, the thought or meaning of the communication will be much clearer.

Weak forms

Certain words in English can have two distinct pronunciations: a strong form and a weak form. Always use the weak forms of these words unless the strong form is needed to change the meaning of the sentence.

AUDIO
18.1

ARTICLES	
WEAK FORM	STRONG FORM
ə a	eĭ a
ə an	æ an
ə the*	i the

PREPOSITIONS	
WEAK FORM	STRONG FORM
ə at	æ at
ɚ for	ɔɚ for
ə from	ʌ from
ə of	ʌ of
ə to	u to
ə into	u into

CONJUNCTIONS	
WEAK FORM	STRONG FORM
ə and	æ and
ə but	ʌ but
ə than	æ than
ɚ or	ɔɚ or
ɚ nor	ɔɚ nor

PRONOUNS	
WEAK FORM	STRONG FORM
ɚ her	ɝ her
ə them	e them
ə us	ʌ us
ɚ your	ʊɚ your
ə some	ʌ some
ə that	æ that

*However, always use ði when the next word begins with a vowel.

AUXILIARY VERBS

WEAK FORM	STRONG FORM	WEAK FORM	STRONG FORM
ə am	æ am	ə has	æ has
ɚ are	ɑɚ are	ə have	æ have
ə can	æ can	ə must	ʌ must
ə could	ʊ could	ə shall	æ shall
ə do	u do	ə should	ʊ should
ə does	ʌ does	ə was	ʌ was
ə had	æ had	ɚ were	ɝ were

Examples of strong forms vs. weak forms

AUDIO 18.2 Read the following examples of weak forms and strong forms aloud. Compare your pronunciation with the recorded examples. Concentrate on distinguishing between weak and strong forms.

from

ʌ
Where are you from?

ə
Bob is from Denver.

of

ʌ
When you're under stress, what do you think of?

ə
Meg dreams of the sea.

for

ɔɚ
Who is the gift for?

ɚ
I bought that for Anne.

but

No "b*u*t"s about it!

I want to swim, b*u*t it's too cold.

some

I don't want all of the pudding, but I want s*o*me.

Mike ate s*o*me fruit.

are

I'm not going out, but they *are*.

Are you sure you're finished?

has

I want what he h*a*s!

He h*a*s a quick wit.

does

Yes, she d*oe*s!

D*oe*s Mary have a cat?

was

Tom w*a*sn't happy, but Ed w*a*s.

I w*a*s about to volunteer.

them

I met with Neil, but not with th<u>e</u>m.
e

We could invite th<u>e</u>m to the party.
ə

Contrasting operative and inoperative words

Following is an exercise in practicing the natural rhythms of English speech. Follow the steps below.

1. Underline all the operative words in a sentence.
2. Cross out all the inoperative words in a sentence.
3. Now, read aloud only the underlined operative words. Notice that they make sense and convey the essential meaning of the sentence without the inoperative words.
4. Finally, read the entire sentence aloud. Notice if this affects the rhythm to which you are normally accustomed.

Just as primary stress within words makes a *syllable* longer, louder, and higher in pitch, so stressing operative words in sentences makes those *words* longer, louder, and higher in pitch. Reading aloud enables you to listen and correct yourself as you work toward a more natural rhythm and flow of English speech.

Sentences

In the following sentences, the operative words are underlined and the inoperative words are crossed out. The weak forms of words are marked with the schwa ə phoneme. Following the steps above, read aloud only the operative words in a sentence, and notice that the thought still makes sense. Then read the entire sentence aloud, giving the inoperative words less stress than the operative words. You will notice an improvement in your intonation. You can check yourself by listening to a recording of these sentences on *Audio Track 18.3.*

AUDIO
18.3

1 Kate ~~would have~~ loved ~~to have~~ gone ~~on~~ vacation.

2 ~~Is it a~~ crime ~~to~~ witness ~~a~~ robbery ~~and~~ say nothing?

3 Pam ~~is a~~ valued colleague ~~as~~ well ~~as the~~ perfect boss.

4 Cheesecake ~~for~~ breakfast—~~are you~~ kidding ~~me~~?

5 Study hard ~~and~~ practice frequently, ~~and you will be~~ sure ~~to~~ see results.

6 ~~Can you~~ believe ~~that~~ another year ~~has~~ gone by so quickly?

7 ~~If~~ raised together, puppies ~~and~~ kittens ~~can be~~ terrific playmates.

8 ~~The~~ first half ~~of the~~ movie ~~was~~ great, ~~but the~~ second half ~~was~~ disappointing.

9 ~~Did you~~ think ~~the~~ fashion show contained clothing lines ~~that were~~ extreme?

10 ~~After a~~ long day's work, I enjoy ~~the~~ company ~~of my~~ friends.

Speaking in phrases and clauses

The last piece in the puzzle of English intonation is to speak in phrases and clauses. A **phrase** is a group of words that may contain nouns and verbs, but it does not have a subject acting on a verb. A **clause** is a group of words that contains a subject that is acting on a verb. Independent clauses can stand on their own as sentences; dependent clauses cannot stand on their own and are secondary thoughts within sentences.

This sounds technical, but the rhythm of English speech is achieved by grouping patterns of words around a central idea. Just as we cautioned against breaking a sentence into individual words, we must also warn against trying to deal with the entire sentence at once. Depending on your past training, you may have been taught to impose an overall sing-song rhythm on English, and indeed, to nonnative speakers, English speech may sound melodious, rhythmic, and fairly arbitrary. But English intonation is actually quite specific: You must distill sentences into phrases and clauses in order to use operative and inoperative words effectively.

The essential communication of a phrase or clause is the expression of an image. In its purest form, the thought of a speaker is condensed into an image or picture that is readily grasped by the listener. This sounds complicated, but is relatively intuitive. Consider the following phrases.

a long day's work
a frisky puppy playing
an abandoned red barn

Each of these phrases probably conjures a definite image in your mind, which will in turn translate into a very specific picture in the minds of your listeners. Consider the following sentence.

After a long day's work, I was reinvigorated by the sight
of a frisky puppy playing in an abandoned red barn.

Now, let's bracket these phrases within the sentence.

[After a long day's work], [I was reinvigorated] by [the sight
of a frisky puppy playing] in [an abandoned red barn].

Notice how much more specific your intonation is by breaking the sentence into phrases, or basic units of thoughts. We can analyze this sentence further by marking the operative and inoperative words, as follows.

[~~After a~~ long day's work], [~~I was~~ reinvigorated] ~~by~~ [~~the~~ sight
~~of a~~ frisky puppy playing] ~~in~~ [~~an~~ abandoned red barn].

Intonation or pitch variance

Many nonnative speakers have been taught that English uses "staircase intonation"—that a speaker should inflect as if lightly bounding down a flight of stairs toward the period at the end of the sentence. But operative words are longer, louder, and higher in pitch, and as you can see in the example above, they generally fall toward the end of phrases and clauses. While native English speakers do inflect downward at the ends of sentences, *the downward inflection occurs only on the final phoneme of the sentence.* If we were to score the pitch in the sentence above, it would look like the following.

[After a ‾‾long day's work‾]‾, [I was ‾‾reinvigorated‾]‾ by [the ‾‾sight‾

of a ‾‾frisky puppy playing‾]‾ in [an ‾‾abandoned red ba‾rn].

It is only the final phoneme that inflects downward, making the statement a declarative sentence. (In this case, it is the r coloring attached to the consonant n.) Similarly, *it is the upward inflection of the final phoneme that turns a statement into a question.* If we were to score the pitch of the interrogative sentence *Would you like some coffee?* it would look like the following.

Would you ‾‾like‾ some ‾‾cof‾fee?

In the sample paragraphs below, the operative words are underlined and the inoperative words are crossed out. The images, or phrases, are bracketed. Read the paragraphs aloud. Notice that the operative words are longer, louder, and higher in pitch than the inoperative words. Remember to inflect downward on the final phoneme of declarative sentences, and to inflect upward on the final phoneme of interrogative sentences.

AUDIO
18.4

The following paragraph is recorded on **Audio Track 18.4**.

Meg and Ed

[Meg ~~and~~ Ed] were [fond ~~of the~~ countryside]. ~~They~~ [loved ~~the~~ fresh air], the [lush foliage], ~~and the~~ [smells ~~and~~ sounds ~~of the~~ outdoors]. However, ~~they were~~ [not fond ~~of~~ exercise], ~~and~~ therefore did [not enjoy hiking]. [One sunny afternoon], ~~they~~ [decided ~~to~~ take a drive ~~through the~~ country]. ~~They~~ [saw a sign advertising fresh produce] ~~and~~ [decided ~~to~~ pull over] ~~and~~ [buy vegetables ~~for~~ dinner]. ~~They~~ [got out ~~of the~~ car] ~~and~~ [went into ~~the~~ small store]. [Ten minutes later], [Meg ~~and~~ Ed emerged ~~with~~ cucumbers, tomatoes, peaches, ~~and~~ pears]. ~~But~~ [when ~~they~~ reached ~~their~~ car], ~~they~~ [discovered one ~~of their~~ tires ~~was~~ flat]. ~~The~~ [nearest gas station] ~~was a~~ [mile away]. Not only ~~did~~ [Meg ~~and~~ Ed purchase delicious produce], ~~they were~~ also [forced ~~to~~ take a hike ~~in the~~ country].

*The following paragraph is recorded on **Audio Track 18.5**.*

Rhonda's vacation

[Rhonda] ~~was~~ [fond ~~of~~ all water sports]. ~~She~~ [enjoyed waterskiing, surfing, ~~and~~ sailing]. ~~But~~ [most ~~of~~ all, ~~she~~ loved ~~to~~ snorkel]. ~~On~~ [one vacation ~~in the~~ Caribbean], ~~she~~ [joined ~~an~~ adventurous tour group] ~~that~~ [rented kayaks] ~~and~~ [paddled across] ~~to a~~ [small deserted island a mile away]. ~~She~~ [put on ~~her~~ mask ~~and~~ flippers] ~~and~~ [dove under ~~the~~ pale blue water]. [Rhonda ~~was~~ astonished] ~~at the~~ [wide variety ~~of~~ fish] ~~and at the~~ [beautiful array ~~of~~ colors surrounding] ~~her, so she~~ [swam out farther] ~~to~~ [continue exploring]. ~~She was~~ [even more astonished ~~an~~ hour later], ~~when she~~ [swam back in] ~~and~~ [found ~~her~~ group ~~had~~ left ~~without her~~]. [Rhonda began ~~to~~ panic]. ~~Her~~ [heart started ~~to~~ race]. ~~Was she~~ [left alone ~~on a~~ deserted island]!? Suddenly, [another group ~~of~~ kayaks] [came ~~around the~~ bend ~~of the~~ cove], ~~and~~ [Rhonda remembered] ~~that there was a~~ [new tour group] ~~that~~ [set off ~~from the~~ hotel every hour].

The same method of scoring can be used for business presentations. Let's turn now to the final chapter of *Perfecting Your English Pronunciation*, and learn how to mark a business speech.

PART FOUR

PUTTING IT ALL TOGETHER

NINETEEN

Marking a business speech

How to prepare for a presentation

Let's take all the lessons from this book and apply them in an organized fashion in order to drastically improve your performance when giving presentations in English.

If you have worked through this book chapter by chapter, you know what your problem sounds are and how to correct them. You also have an understanding of operative and inoperative words and of speaking in phrases and clauses to allow your listeners to better image the content of your communication. To prepare for your presentation, print out a copy of it (double spaced, so you have space for your marks) and grab a pencil. Let's get started.

Step 1: Marking difficult sounds

Begin by marking all of your difficult sounds. Put the phonetic symbols for these challenging sounds directly above their English spelling equivalents. Following are three examples of Fred's business pitches, with problem sounds marked phonetically.

Fred's business pitch No. 1
(marked for the sounds ð/θ, r, ɪ, and oŭ/ɑ)

  ð   ɑ oŭ ɪ   r   ɑ   r
The following PowerPoint presentation on your computer screen

  oŭ ɪ ɑ r ɪ   ɪ r   oŭoŭ   r oŭ
focuses on creating a different portfolio scenario for your client's

  ɪ ɪ   ɪ ɪ ɪ   ɪ   ɪ   ɑ ɪ   r   ɑ
dividends. It is examined using an economic deceleration model,

     ɪ ɪ   ɪ ɑ ð   ɪ   r   ɪ   ɪ
as delineated on the accompanying spreadsheets. In our opinion,

        ɑ   ɪ ɪ   ɪ   ɪ   ɪ   ɪ r
your client's company stock dividends will be impacted and increase

  r   ɪ   ɪ ð ɪ   oŭoŭ r   ɪ ɪ   ɪ ɪ ð
dramatically if this portfolio structure is implemented in the next

 ɪ   θ   ɪ   ð   ɪ   ɪ   ɪ   ɪ ɪ
six months. We believe that your client's business is *our* business.

         ɪ   ɪ ɳ   r   r
We are Universal Securities Trust—"US Trust." And we can assure

 ð   ɪ
that you *will*.

AUDIO
19.1

Now, mark this business pitch with any additional sounds with which you have difficulty. Then, *turn to **Audio Track 19.1*** and listen to a recording of Fred's business pitch No. 1. Record yourself reading the pitch above, and compare your pronunciation with that on the audio track.

Fred's business pitch No. 2
(marked for the sounds *l, ʤ, b/v/w, ʌ,* and *ʊ*)

    v   l   ʊ   ʌ w   ʌ   ʤ   l
Universal Securities Trust wants you to understand the generally

          v ʊ   l   ʌ   ʌ   w
enduring effect of putting together a portfolio structure underweighted

        l ʌ   ʊ   v
in a few financial companies. The good news is that moving towards

       ʌ   w l   bl   l   v lʊ
a new structure will indisputably increase cash flow. A positive outlook

   l   v bʊl   ʊ   ʤ   l
until the return of a bull market should re-energize employee

    ʌ v w   ʌ ʤʌ ʌ ʌ lʊ
productivity. We're US Trust—just trust us to look out for you!

AUDIO 19.2 Now, mark this business pitch with any additional sounds with which you have difficulty. Then, *turn to **Audio Track 19.2*** and listen to a recording of Fred's business pitch No. 2. Record yourself reading the pitch above, and compare your pronunciation with that on the audio track.

Fred's business pitch No. 3
(marked for the sounds ð/θ, r, ŋ, e, æ, and ɔ)

                        ŋ   e ð   ɔ   r   r e
Your accounting shows a less than plausible return for projected

re   æ   r ŋ   æ   æ
revenues, and due to a lack of operating cash flow, we cannot

re   e   ð   ɔ   æ   ɔ θ r   ŋ
recommend that you automatically authorize complete funding

      ð   e   e   r
on these new ventures. However, if you will allow Universal Securities

r   ɔ   ð   ð rɔ   ɔ ð
Trust to halt further withdrawals and overhaul these accounts

    ð   r   ɔ   æ   e r
with a proper audit, we *can* assure you of a positive outcome. US Trust—

r
trust us!

AUDIO 19.3 Now, mark this business pitch with any additional sounds with which you have difficulty. Then, *turn to **Audio Track 19.3*** and listen to a recording of Fred's business pitch No. 3. Record yourself reading the pitch above, and compare your pronunciation with that on the audio track.

Step 2: Marking operative and inoperative words

Now, we'll mark the same three business pitches for operative and inoperative words. To better highlight the images in the pitches, we'll also bracket the phrases and clauses.

Fred's business pitch No. 1

~~The~~ [following PowerPoint presentation] ~~on your~~ [computer screen] [focuses ~~on~~ creating ~~a~~ different portfolio scenario] ~~for your~~ [client's dividends]. [~~It is~~ examined] [using ~~an~~ economic deceleration model],

~~as~~ [delineated ~~on the~~ accompanying spreadsheets]. [~~In our~~ opinion], ~~your~~ [client's company stock dividends] ~~will be~~ [impacted] ~~and~~ [increase dramatically] ~~if this~~ [portfolio structure] ~~is~~ [implemented] ~~in the~~ [next six months]. ~~We~~ [believe] ~~that your~~ [client's business] ~~is~~ [*our* business]. ~~We are~~ [Universal Securities Trust]—["US Trust"]. ~~And we can~~ [assure ~~that you~~ *will*].

Fred's business pitch No. 2

[Universal Securities Trust] [wants ~~you to~~ understand] ~~the~~ [generally enduring effect] ~~of~~ [putting together a portfolio structure] [underweighted] ~~in a~~ [few financial companies]. ~~The~~ [good news] ~~is that~~ [moving ~~towards a~~ new structure] ~~will~~ [indisputably increase cash flow]. ~~A~~ [positive outlook] ~~until the~~ [return ~~of a~~ bull market] ~~should~~ [re-energize employee productivity]. ~~We're~~ [US Trust]— [just trust us ~~to~~ look out ~~for you~~]!

Fred's business pitch No. 3

[~~Your~~ accounting] [shows ~~a less than~~ plausible return] ~~for~~ [projected revenues], ~~and~~ [due ~~to a~~ lack ~~of~~ operating cash flow], ~~we~~ [cannot recommend] ~~that you~~ [automatically authorize complete funding] ~~on these~~ [new ventures]. However, ~~if you will~~ [allow Universal Securities Trust] ~~to~~ [halt further withdrawals] ~~and~~ [overhaul ~~these~~ accounts] ~~with a~~ [proper audit], ~~we~~ [*can* assure] ~~you of a~~ [positive outcome]. [US Trust]—[trust us]!

Further practice

Now, let's work on the more advanced business presentations below. After you have practiced with these sample presentations, you can apply the same steps to your own business text.

Business sample No. 1: The impact of the economic crisis on insurance companies

Begin by marking all of your difficult sounds in the paragraphs below. Underline the consonant and vowel sounds that you find challenging, then mark their phonetic symbol equivalents above.

The first text is scored for operative and inoperative words. Phrases and clauses are bracketed to highlight the desired imaging of the speaker.

[Most insurers] have [suffered the impact] of [depressed equity prices] and of [low long-term yields]. Even the [best-prepared companies] have had to [reinforce their hedging strategies] and are [currently dealing] with [unprecedented volatility in their stock prices]. We are [still in a phase] where [volatility is largely driven] by the [market's fears regarding solvency].

But [looking beyond] the [immediate market volatility], it is [clear] that there is ["real economy" damage]. This is [already starting to have an impact] on the [insurance industry]. We can [predict with some certainty] that [customer demand] will [decline sharply]. [Insurers] will [need to be clear] about the [markets] and [product areas] that will [continue to thrive] and that [deserve strong investment], those that will [decline temporarily], and those that [present an opportunity] ~~for~~ [long-term share gains] ~~in~~ [exchange] ~~for~~ [short-term pain].

[Recessions] [always create opportunities] ~~to~~ [reshape ~~the~~ competitive landscape]. ~~The~~ [insurance industry] ~~is~~ [generally better prepared] [this time around]. ~~But the~~ [double impact] ~~of the~~ [financial crisis] ~~and the~~ [damage ~~on~~ consumer demand] mean ~~that~~ [this downturn] ~~will be~~ [no exception].

AUDIO

19.4

*Now listen to **Audio Track 19.4**. The speaker is a native of Thailand, and there are two recordings—"before" and "after" versions of Business sample No. 1. The second recording was made after learning and using the *Perfecting Your English Pronunciation* method.

Business sample No. 2: Strategy in the information systems business

Begin by marking all of your difficult sounds in the paragraph below. Underline the consonant and vowel sounds that you find challenging, then mark their phonetic symbol equivalents above.

Next, score this second text for operative and inoperative words, and bracket phrases and clauses to highlight the desired imaging of the speaker.

Let's focus on the information systems business. The issues are real.

Our company can leverage a powerful mix of technologies for the information systems. Yet other subsidiary companies—parts suppliers, electronics companies, content providers, and airtime providers— are all fighting for dominant positions in the same space. Major growth in information systems is certain—who will capture that growth is not at all clear. For our company, the information systems business represents a wonderful opportunity amidst great uncertainty and change. In the end, we must together define the core value at which our company excels, the currency that will cause partners to sign up for this integrated business model to serve the consumer. To speed our company's race towards the marketplace, and to more clearly define a strategy, we will use external interviews, internal interviews, and objective data to establish the value that each type of player brings at positions along the value chain.

AUDIO
19.5

*Now listen to **Audio Track 19.5**.* The speaker is of Hispanic descent, and there are two recordings—"before" and "after" versions of Business sample No. 2. The second recording was made after learning and using the *Perfecting Your English Pronunciation* method.

Business sample No. 3: Valuation financial model

Begin by marking all of your difficult sounds in the paragraphs below. Underline the consonant and vowel sounds that you find challenging, then mark their phonetic symbol equivalents above.

Next, score this third text for operative and inoperative words, and bracket phrases and clauses to highlight the desired imaging of the speaker.

This model is a vehicle for comparing the results of your company's valuation methodology with the historical share prices of other companies under analysis. Previously, viewing the effect on share price tracking was laborious and time-consuming. Now, using this tool, your company can perform this analysis quickly. This model also allows analysis on an unlimited number of departments simultaneously, rather than one by one.

It is important to note that this model is designed for use with financial services companies. Thus, the growth rates used to create spot valuations are those of equity, not assets, and the return measure is return on equity, not return on investment. Adapting the model for use with industrial companies should not be difficult, but in its present incarnation, it applies to banks.

AUDIO

19.6

Now listen to **Audio Track 19.6**. The speaker is a native of India, and there are two recordings—"before" and "after" versions of Business sample No. 3. The second recording was made after learning and using the *Perfecting Your English Pronunciation* method.

Scoring your presentations

You can use the following system to score all your presentations.

Step one

To "zero in on" your pronunciation problems, mark all of your difficult sounds on the presentation. If you are not certain which vowel sounds to choose, check the spelling patterns and word lists in Chapters Three through Sixteen. Underline the consonant and vowel sounds that you find challenging, then mark their phonetic symbol equivalents above.

Step two

Underline the operative words in the presentation and cross out the inoperative words. Read only the operative words. Notice that they make sense on their own; this will enable you to bracket the images. Now, bracket phrases and clauses to highlight your desired imaging.

Step three

Read the presentation once again, adding the inoperative words. This not only dramatically improves your intonation, it makes your thoughts much clearer to your listeners.

Always remember: Try to relax. Most people speak much more quickly when nervous. This was an ongoing problem for Fred, but he found that bracketing his thoughts on paper helped him slow down and let the images resonate with his audience.

Fred, by the way, is a composite of all students who have used the Cameron Method of Accent Modification®, with *Perfecting Your English Pronunciation*. The name stands for **FR**ustrated with **E**nglish **D**iction. Fred is *you*. And Fred is frustrated no longer!

Prefixes, suffixes, and common word endings with ɪ

As indicated in Chapter Nine, the vowel ɪ is generally spelled with *i* or *y*. There are exceptions, however. When the letter *e* is used in the unstressed first syllable of a word (often a prefix like *de-*, *ex-*, and *re-*), it is pronounced ɪ. Following are common words that use the ɪ sound in this way.

PREFIX ɪ WITH *e* SPELLING PATTERN

because	emerge	reform
become	enjoy	release
before	exposed	relief
began	express	response
debate	extend	result
decide	extent	resume
declare	extreme	retain
decline	precise	retire
defeat	prefer	return
describe	prepare	reveal
design	receive	review
desire	reduce	select
effect	refer	
elect	reflect	

In addition, there are seven suffixes and other common word endings that use the ɪ vowel but are not spelled with *i*: *-age*, *-ate* (as a noun or adjective, but not as a verb), *-ed*, *-es*, *-ess*, *-est*, and *-et*. Following are common words that use these suffixes and common word endings.

269

SUFFIX -*age*

advant_age_	dam_age_	pack_age_
aver_age_	encour_age_	pass_age_
bever_age_	im_age_	percent_age_
carri_age_	langu_age_	sav_age_
cott_age_	man_age_	sew_age_
cour_age_	marri_age_	stor_age_
cover_age_	mess_age_	vill_age_

SUFFIX -*ate*

accur_ate_	doctor_ate_
adequ_ate_	elaborate (*adjective*)
appropri_ate_ (*adjective*)	estim_ate_ (*noun*)
approxim_ate_ (*adjective*)	fortun_ate_
articul_ate_ (*adjective*)	gradu_ate_ (*noun, adjective*)
associ_ate_ (*noun, adjective*)	illegitim_ate_
candid_ate_*	immedi_ate_
clim_ate_	intim_ate_ (*noun, adjective*)
corpor_ate_	legitim_ate_ (*adjective*)
deliber_ate_ (*adjective*)	moder_ate_ (*noun, adjective*)
delic_ate_	separ_ate_ (*adjective*)
desper_ate_	ultim_ate_

SUFFIX -*ed*

add_ed_	nodd_ed_	shout_ed_
grant_ed_	not_ed_	sound_ed_
greet_ed_	paint_ed_	start_ed_
guid_ed_	point_ed_	stat_ed_
hand_ed_	print_ed_	treat_ed_
hundr_ed_	quot_ed_	vot_ed_
lift_ed_	sacr_ed_	wait_ed_
need_ed_	seat_ed_	want_ed_

---

*The *a* of the suffix of this word may also be pronounced eĭ.

SUFFIX -*es*

blesses	lashes	passes
causes	misses	thrashes
dresses	noses	wishes

SUFFIX -*ess*

business	happiness	regardless
consciousness	helpless	stillness
darkness	illness	thickness
endless	reckless	weakness

SUFFIX -*est*

biggest	honest	modest
greatest	interest	nearest
forest	latest	prettiest
highest	longest	strongest

SUFFIX -*et*

blanket	jacket	quiet
budget	market	secret
bullet	planet	target
cricket	pocket	ticket
diet	poet	

Pronunciation of final *s*: *s* or *z*?

Nonnative speakers of English are often confused about how to pronounce the letter *s*: as a voiceless s or as a voiced z? Unfortunately, *s* can be either voiceless or voiced, independent of spelling patterns. However, there are three instances in English in which *s* is added to an existing word.

> To make a noun plural
> To make a noun possessive
> To make the third-person singular form of a present-tense verb

In these three instances, a simple rule dictates whether the *s* is voiceless or voiced. When adding *s*, look at the sound that precedes it. If the sound is voiceless, the *s* is voiceless; if the sound is voiced, the *s* is voiced.

Note, however, that if the word ends in a sibilant (s, z, ʃ, ʒ, ʧ, or ʤ), whether voiced or voiceless, the suffix is -*es* (or *'s* for possessives) and is pronounced ɪz.

Examples

Many team**s** compete, but not all win pennant**s**.

Kirk'**s** dog is ten year**s** old. Anne'**s** is still a puppy.

After Matt work**s** out at the gym, he run**s** a mile.

Fred wishe**s** that Thomas'**s** speeche**s** were shorter.

273

Video and audio contents by track

The streaming video and audio that accompany this book are accessed via the McGraw-Hill Education Language Lab app. See inside cover and mhlanguagelab.com for more details. (Internet access required.)

Video track numbers and titles are followed by corresponding book page numbers.

Audio track numbers and titles are followed by corresponding book page numbers.

About the author

Susan Cameron is a specialist in accent modification and has taught thousands of students and professionals from all over the world. She was granted a trademark by the U.S. government for the Cameron Method of Accent Modification®, which highlights her use of hand positions to sync the articulators of speech and find the precise physical placement of English pronunciation. This is the second edition of *Perfecting Your English Pronunciation*. A computer-animated version of this content, entitled *Perfect English Pronunciation* has also been rendered as an app and released on IOS and Android. Susan's television/radio appearances include interviews on Sinovision (China), NHK-TV (Japan), and NPR radio (USA).

Susan is also a professional dialect coach in theater, television, and film. As an educator, she currently is on the full-time faculty at Columbia University School of the Arts, as well as an adjunct Associate Professor at The New School for Drama. Former teaching positions include adjunct Associate Professor at New York University's Tisch Graduate Acting Program and Master Teacher and Chair of Voice and Speech at NYU Tisch School of the Arts CAP21 program, among others. Susan holds a Master of Fine Arts degree from Yale University.